JUMP Math 6.2

Book 6 Part 2 of 2

M000011487

Contents

Unit 1: The Number System	1
Unit 2: Ratios and Proportional Relationships	41
Unit 3: Expressions and Equations	61
Unit 4: The Number System	78
Unit 5: Geometry	92
Unit 6: Expressions and Equations	110
Unit 7: Statistics and Probability	122
Unit 8: Geometry	132
Unit 9: Statistics and Probability	155

jump math™

MULTIPLYING POTENTIAL.

JUMP Math
One Yonge Street, Suite 1014
Toronto, Ontario M5E 1E5
Canada
www.jumpmath.org

Writers: Dr. John Mighton, Dr. Sindi Sabourin, Dr. Anna Klebanov, Dr. Sohrab Rahbar, Julie Lorinc
Editors: Dimitra Chronopoulos, Debbie Davies-Wright, Ewa Krynski
Layout and Illustrations: Linh Lam, Gabriella Kerr
Cover Design: Blakeley Words+Pictures
Cover Photograph: © iStockphoto.com/Grafissimo

ISBN 978-1-927457-07-8

First printing July 2013

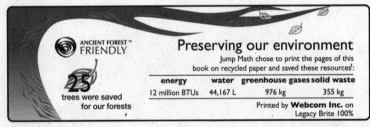

Preserving our environment
Jump Math chose to print the pages of this book on recycled paper and saved these resources[1]:

energy	water	greenhouse gases	solid waste
12 million BTUs	44,167 L	976 kg	355 kg

Printed by **Webcom Inc.** on Legacy Brite 100%

25 trees were saved for our forests

RECYCLED
100%
RECYCLABLE
Legacy Brite 100%

Printed by **Webcom Inc.**

[1]Estimates were made using the Environmental Defense Paper Calculator.

This book was manufactured without the use of additional coatings or processes, and was assembled using the latest equipment to achieve almost zero waste. Manufacturing this book in Canada ensures compliance with strict environmental practices and eliminates the need for international freight, which is a major contributor to global air pollution.

Printed and bound in Canada

Welcome to JUMP Math

Entering the world of JUMP Math means believing that every child has the capacity to be fully numerate and to love math. Founder and mathematician John Mighton has used this premise to develop his innovative teaching method. The resulting resources isolate and describe concepts so clearly and incrementally that everyone can understand them.

JUMP Math is comprised of teacher's guides (which are the heart of our program), interactive whiteboard lessons, student assessment & practice books, evaluation materials, outreach programs, and teacher training. The Common Core Editions of our resources have been carefully designed to cover the Common Core State Standards. All of this is presented on the JUMP Math website: **www.jumpmath.org**.

Teacher's guides are available on the website for free use. Read the introduction to the teacher's guides before you begin using these resources. This will ensure that you understand both the philosophy and the methodology of JUMP Math. The assessment & practice books are designed for use by students, with adult guidance. Each student will have unique needs and it is important to provide the student with the appropriate support and encouragement as he or she works through the material.

Allow students to discover the concepts by themselves as much as possible. Mathematical discoveries can be made in small, incremental steps. The discovery of a new step is like untangling the parts of a puzzle. It is exciting and rewarding.

Children will need to answer the questions marked with a ▯ in a notebook. Grid paper notebooks should always be on hand for answering extra questions or when additional room for calculation is needed.

Contents

PART 1

Unit 1: Ratios and Proportional Relationships

RP6-1	Sequences	1
RP6-2	Extending a Sequence	3
RP6-3	Tables	4
RP6-4	Multiplying and Dividing by Skip Counting	7
RP6-5	Mental Math and the Standard Method for Multiplication	9
RP6-6	Introduction to Ratios	12
RP6-7	Introduction to Ratio Tables	13
RP6-8	Unit Rates	15
RP6-9	Finding Unit Rates	17
RP6-10	Double Number Line Diagrams	18

Unit 2: The Number System

NS6-1	Place Value	19
NS6-2	Representation in Expanded Form	22
NS6-3	Integers	24
NS6-4	Opposite Integers	27
NS6-5	Comparing Multi-Digit Integers	28
NS6-6	Models of Fractions	30
NS6-7	Comparing Positive and Negative Fractions	32
NS6-8	Mixed Numbers and Improper Fractions	34
NS6-9	Fractions on a Number Line	37
NS6-10	More Mixed Numbers and Improper Fractions	38
NS6-11	Comparing Fractions on a Number Line	41
NS6-12	Equivalent Fractions	43
NS6-13	Equivalent Negative Fractions	46
NS6-14	Lowest Common Multiples (LCMs)	47
NS6-15	Factors	50
NS6-16	Greatest Common Factors (GCFs)	53
NS6-17	Greatest Common Factors (Advanced)	55
NS6-18	Counterexamples	57
NS6-19	Problems and Puzzles (Advanced)	59
NS6-20	Comparing Fractions Using Equivalent Fractions	61
NS6-21	Applying LCMs and GCFs to Fractions	63
NS6-22	Adding and Subtracting Mixed Numbers	66
NS6-23	More Problems and Puzzles	69

Unit 3: Expressions and Equations

EE6-1	Numerical Expressions	71
EE6-2	Unknown Quantities	72
EE6-3	Variables	74
EE6-4	Modeling Equations	76
EE6-5	Solving Equations with Balances	77
EE6-6	Solving Equations—Guess and Check	79
EE6-7	Equations Involving Fractions	80

Unit 4: The Number System

NS6-24	Decimal Fractions	82
NS6-25	Place Value and Decimals	85
NS6-26	Positive and Negative Decimals	88
NS6-27	Equivalent Fractions and Decimals	91
NS6-28	Ordering Decimals	93
NS6-29	Comparing Decimal Fractions and Decimals	95
NS6-30	Comparing Fractions and Decimals	97
NS6-31	Multi-Digit Addition	99
NS6-32	Multi-Digit Subtraction	102
NS6-33	Adding and Subtracting Decimals	105
NS6-34	Rounding	109
NS6-35	Rounding Decimals	111
NS6-36	Decimals Review	114
NS6-37	Fractions of a Whole Number	116
NS6-38	Multiplying Fractions by Whole Numbers	118
NS6-39	Multiplying Decimals by Powers of 10	120
NS6-40	Multiplying and Dividing by Powers of 10	123
NS6-41	Multiplying Decimals by Whole Numbers	125

Unit 5: Ratios and Proportional Relationships

RP6-11	Equivalent Ratios	126
RP6-12	Finding Equivalent Ratios	127
RP6-13	Percents	129
RP6-14	Visual Representation of Percents	131
RP6-15	Comparing Decimals, Fractions, and Percents	133
RP6-16	Long Multiplication (Review)	134
RP6-17	Finding Percents	136
RP6-18	Finding Percents Using Multiplication	137
RP6-19	Percents: Word Problems	138
RP6-20	Fractions, Ratios, and Percents	139
RP6-21	Long Division (Review)	142
RP6-22	Long Division and Unit Rates	145

Unit 6: Geometry

G6-1	Polygons (Review)	147
G6-2	Special Quadrilaterals	149
G6-3	Parallel Lines on a Grid	152
G6-4	Coordinate Systems	153
G6-5	Horizontal and Vertical Distance	156
G6-6	Ratios and Coordinate Systems	157
G6-7	Area of Rectangles	159
G6-8	Area and Perimeter	161
G6-9	Area of Composite Shapes	162
G6-10	Area of Parallelograms	164
G6-11	Area of Triangles	166
G6-12	Area of Triangles and Parallelograms	168
G6-13	Area of Trapezoids and Parallelograms	170
G6-14	Organizing Data	172
G6-15	Variables and Area	174
G6-16	Comparing Units of Length	176
G6-17	Changing Units of Length	178
G6-18	Changing Units and Using Formulas	180
G6-19	Problems with Area	182

PART 2
Unit 1: The Number System

NS6-42	Order of Operations	1
NS6-43	Properties of Operations	3
NS6-44	Powers	5
NS6-45	Division with Fractional Answers	7
NS6-46	Division, Fractions, and Decimals	9
NS6-47	Multiplying Fractions	10
NS6-48	Multiplying Decimals by Decimals	13
NS6-49	Dividing Fractions by Whole Numbers	15
NS6-50	Dividing Whole Numbers by Unit Fractions	16
NS6-51	Dividing Fractions by Unit Fractions	18
NS6-52	Dividing Whole Numbers by Fractions (Introduction)	20
NS6-53	Dividing 1 by a Fraction	21
NS6-54	Dividing by Fractions	23
NS6-55	Word Problems (Advanced)	26
NS6-56	Fractions and Order of Operations (Advanced)	27
NS6-57	Dividing Decimals by Whole Numbers	29
NS6-58	Dividing by Decimals	31
NS6-59	2-Digit Division (Introduction)	33

NS6-60	2-Digit Division	35
NS6-61	2-Digit Division—Guess and Check	37
NS6-62	Cumulative Review	39

Unit 2: Ratios and Proportional Relationships

RP6-23	Ratios and Rates with Fractional Terms	41
RP6-24	Unit Rates with Fractional and Decimal Terms	44
RP6-25	Proportions and Word Problems	46
RP6-26	Using Unit Rates to Solve Problems	48
RP6-27	Changing US Customary Units of Length	50
RP6-28	Using Unit Rates to Convert Measurements	52
RP6-29	Tape Diagrams	54
RP6-30	Writing Equivalent Statements for Proportions	56
RP6-31	Cumulative Review	58

Unit 3: Expressions and Equations

EE6-8	Solving Equations—Preserving Equality	61
EE6-9	Solving Equations—Using Logic	63
EE6-10	Totals, Differences, and Equations	65
EE6-11	Addition and Subtraction World Problems	68
EE6-12	Models and "Times as Many"	70
EE6-13	Evaluating Expressions	72
EE6-14	Multiplication Equations and Word Problems	74
EE6-15	More Multistep Word Problems	76

Unit 4: The Number System

NS6-63	Opposite Values	78
NS6-64	Debits, Credits, and Debt	80
NS6-65	The Meaning of Zero	82
NS6-66	Opposite Integers Again	84
NS6-67	Distance Apart	85
NS6-68	Absolute Value	87
NS6-69	Concepts in Absolute Value	89

Unit 5: Geometry

G6-20	The Four Quadrants of a Coordinate Grid	92
G6-21	Coordinate Systems	95
G6-22	Horizontal and Vertical Lines	97
G6-23	Distance on Horizontal and Vertical Lines	98
G6-24	Using Distance to Identify Shapes	100
G6-25	Quadrilaterals on Coordinate Grids	102

G6-26	Area on Coordinate Grids	103
G6-27	Reflections	105
G6-28	Reflections (Advanced)	107
G6-29	Applications of Coordinate Grids	108

Unit 6: Expressions and Equations

EE6-16	Equivalent Expressions	110
EE6-17	Solving Algebraic Equations	112
EE6-18	Word Problems	114
EE6-19	Graphs and Equations	116
EE6-20	Dependent and Independent Variables	118
EE6-21	Introduction to Inequalities	120

Unit 7: Statistics and Probability

SP6-1	Mean	122
SP6-2	Mean, Median, and Range	126
SP6-3	Frequency	128
SP6-4	Dot Plots	129

Unit 8: Geometry

G6-30	Stacking Blocks	132
G6-31	Volume	134
G6-32	Volume of Boxes with Fractional Sides	136
G6-33	Concepts in Volume	138
G6-34	Vertices, Edges, and Faces	140
G6-35	Prisms and Pyramids	142
G6-36	Parallel and Perpendicular Edges and Faces	144
G6-37	Surface Area of Rectangular Prisms	145
G6-38	Nets	147
G6-39	Nets and Surface Area of Rectangular Prisms	150
G6-40	Surface Area of Prisms and Pyramids	152
G6-41	Volume and Surface Area (Advanced)	153

Unit 9: Statistics and Probability

SP6-5	Histograms	155
SP6-6	Mean Absolute Deviation	157
SP6-7	Interquartile Range	159
SP6-8	Box Plots	162
SP6-9	Distributions	164

NS6-42 Order of Operations

1. **a)** Add the same numbers two ways. Do the addition in brackets first.

  i) $(4 + 6) + 5$ $4 + (6 + 5)$ ii) $(3 + 7) + 2$ $3 + (7 + 2)$

  $= \underline{\hspace{1cm}} + 5$ $= 4 + \underline{\hspace{1cm}}$ $= \underline{\hspace{1cm}} + \underline{\hspace{1cm}}$ $= \underline{\hspace{1cm}} + \underline{\hspace{1cm}}$

  $= \underline{\hspace{1cm}}$ $= \underline{\hspace{1cm}}$ $= \underline{\hspace{1cm}}$ $= \underline{\hspace{1cm}}$

  b) Does the answer change depending on which addition you do first? $\underline{\hspace{1.5cm}}$

2. **a)** Subtract the same numbers two ways. Do the subtraction in brackets first.

  i) $(7 - 4) - 2$ $7 - (4 - 2)$ ii) $10 - (4 - 3)$ $(10 - 4) - 3$

  $= \underline{\hspace{1cm}} - \underline{\hspace{1cm}}$ $= \underline{\hspace{1cm}} - \underline{\hspace{1cm}}$ $= \underline{\hspace{1cm}} - \underline{\hspace{1cm}}$ $= \underline{\hspace{1cm}} - \underline{\hspace{1cm}}$

  $= \underline{\hspace{1cm}}$ $= \underline{\hspace{1cm}}$ $= \underline{\hspace{1cm}}$ $= \underline{\hspace{1cm}}$

  b) Does the answer change depending on which subtraction you do first? $\underline{\hspace{1.5cm}}$

> Add and subtract in the order you read: from left to right.

3. Add or subtract from left to right.

  a) $7 + 3 - 2$ **b)** $7 - 3 + 2$ **c)** $8 + 4 + 2$ **d)** $10 - 4 - 3$

  $= 10 - 2$

  $= 8$

> Multiplication and division are also done from left to right.

4. Multiply or divide from left to right.

  a) $4 \times 3 \div 6$ **b)** $8 \div 2 \times 5$ **c)** $10 \times 2 \times 3$ **d)** $24 \div 2 \div 3$

> When evaluating expressions, first do all multiplications and divisions from left to right.
> Then do all additions and subtractions from left to right.

5. Circle the operation you would do first.

  a) $3 + \boxed{4 \times 2}$ **b)** $10 - 3 + 4$ **c)** $8 + 2 \div 2$ **d)** $12 - 6 \div 3$

  e) $8 \div 4 \times 3$ **f)** $8 - 2 \times 3$ **g)** $7 + 3 - 4$ **h)** $8 \times 3 - 4$

  i) $15 \div 3 + 2$ **j)** $12 \div 6 - 2$ **k)** $5 \times 4 + 3$ **l)** $5 \times 4 \div 2$

6. Which operation is done first? Do it, then rewrite the rest of the expression.

a) $7 + 4 - 3$

$= \underline{\quad 11 - 3 \quad}$

b) $6 + 4 \div 2$

$= \underline{\quad 6 + 2 \quad}$

c) $10 \div 2 + 3$

$= \underline{\qquad\qquad}$

d) $12 \div 3 \times 2$

$= \underline{\qquad\qquad}$

e) $12 - 7 - 4$

$= \underline{\qquad\qquad}$

f) $3 \times 4 \div 2$

$= \underline{\qquad\qquad}$

g) $8 \div 4 - 2$

$= \underline{\qquad\qquad}$

h) $8 - 3 + 2$

$= \underline{\qquad\qquad}$

i) $3 \times 20 \div 10$

$= \underline{\qquad\qquad}$

If there are brackets in an expression, do the operations in brackets first.

Example: $7 - 3 + 2 = 4 + 2$ but $7 - (3 + 2) = 7 - 5$

$= 6$ $= 2$

---

7. Do the operation in brackets first. Then write the answer.

a) $10 + (4 \times 2)$

$= 10 + 8$

$= 18$

b) $(10 + 4) \times 2$

c) $(10 + 4) \div 2$

d) $10 + (4 \div 2)$

e) $10 - (4 \times 2)$

f) $(10 - 4) \times 2$

g) $(10 - 4) \div 2$

h) $10 - (4 \div 2)$

i) $12 \times (3 \times 2)$

j) $(12 \times 3) \times 2$

k) $(8 \div 4) \div 2$

l) $8 \div (4 \div 2)$

To avoid writing brackets all the time, mathematicians use a standard **order of operations**:

1. Do operations in brackets.
2. Do all multiplications and divisions from left to right.
3. Do all additions and subtractions from left to right.

---

8. Do the operations one at a time, in the standard order.

a) $10 \div 2 \times (5 - 2)$

$= \underline{\quad 10 \div 2 \times 3 \quad}$

$= \underline{\quad 5 \times 3 \quad}$

$= \underline{\quad 15 \quad}$

b) $(9 + 12) \div 3 \times 2$

$= \underline{\qquad\qquad}$

$= \underline{\qquad\qquad}$

$= \underline{\qquad\qquad}$

c) $(13 - 3) \div (7 - 2)$

$= \underline{\qquad\qquad}$

$= \underline{\qquad\qquad}$

$= \underline{\qquad\qquad}$

NS6-43 Properties of Operations

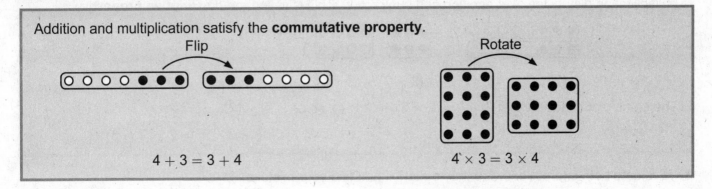

Addition and multiplication satisfy the **commutative property**.

Flip

Rotate

$4 + 3 = 3 + 4$

$4 \times 3 = 3 \times 4$

1. a) Draw a picture to show how $2 + 5 = 5 + 2$.　　　b) Draw a picture to show how $2 \times 5 = 5 \times 2$.

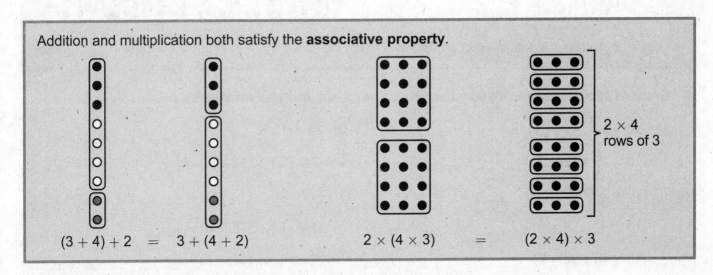

Addition and multiplication both satisfy the **associative property**.

2×4 rows of 3

$(3 + 4) + 2 \;=\; 3 + (4 + 2)$　　　　$2 \times (4 \times 3) \;=\; (2 \times 4) \times 3$

2. Evaluate both expressions. Are they equal? If not, find your mistake.

a) $(3 + 4) + 5 =$ _____ $+ 5 =$ _____

$3 + (4 + 5) = 3 +$ _____ $=$ _____

b) $(3 \times 4) \times 5 =$ _____ $\times 5 =$ _____

$3 \times (4 \times 5) = 3 \times$ _____ $=$ _____

c) $(2 + 5) + 8 =$ _____ $+$ _____ $=$ _____

$2 + (5 + 8) =$ _____ $+$ _____ $=$ _____

d) $(2 \times 5) \times 8 =$ _____ $\times$ _____ $=$ _____

$2 \times (5 \times 8) =$ _____ $\times$ _____ $=$ _____

e) $(3 + 3) + 8 =$ _____ $+$ _____ $=$ _____

$3 + (3 + 8) =$ _____ $+$ _____ $=$ _____

f) $(2 \times 3) \times 3 =$ _____ $\times$ _____ $=$ _____

$2 \times (3 \times 3) =$ _____ $\times$ _____ $=$ _____

Multiplication distributes over addition and subtraction. This is called the **distributive property**.

 =

$$2 \times (3 + 4) \qquad = \qquad (2 \times 3) + (2 \times 4)$$

The same pictures show that $2 \times 7 = (2 \times 3) + (2 \times 4)$, so $(2 \times 7) - (2 \times 3) = 2 \times 4$

$$= 2 \times (7 - 3)$$

3. Evaluate both expressions. Are they equal? If not, find your mistake.

a) $5 \times (2 + 4) = 5 \times$ _____ = _____

$(5 \times 2) + (5 \times 4) =$ _____ + _____ = _____

b) $(3 + 2) \times 4 =$ _____ $\times 4 =$ _____

$(3 \times 4) + (2 \times 4) =$ _____ + _____ = _____

c) $3 \times (7 - 5) = 3 \times$ _____ = _____

$(3 \times 7) - (3 \times 5) =$ _____ - _____ = _____

d) $(9 - 3) \times 5 =$ _____ $\times$ _____ = _____

$(9 \times 5) - (3 \times 5) =$ _____ - _____ = _____

8 dots ÷ 2 groups = 4 dots in each group (8×3) dots ÷ (2×3) groups = 4 dots in each group

4. Evaluate all expressions. Are your answers equal? If not, find your mistake(s).

a) $10 \div 2 =$ _____

$(10 \times 2) \div (2 \times 2) =$ _____ ÷ _____ = _____

$(10 \times 3) \div (2 \times 3) =$ _____ ÷ _____ = _____

$(10 \times 4) \div (2 \times 4) =$ _____ ÷ _____ = _____

$(10 \times 5) \div (2 \times 5) =$ _____ ÷ _____ = _____

b) $24 \div 12 =$ _____

$(24 \div 2) \div (12 \div 2) =$ _____ ÷ _____ = _____

$(24 \div 3) \div (12 \div 3) =$ _____ ÷ _____ = _____

$(24 \div 4) \div (12 \div 4) =$ _____ ÷ _____ = _____

$(24 \div 6) \div (12 \div 6) =$ _____ ÷ _____ = _____

5. Which property does the equation show? Write the correct letter in the blank.

A. the commutative property   **B.** the associative property   **C.** the distributive property

a) $3 \times 4 = 4 \times 3$ _____

b) $3 \times (4 + 5) = 3 \times 4 + 3 \times 5$ _____

c) $3 + (6 + 4) = (3 + 6) + 4$ _____

d) $132 + 4 = 4 + 132$ _____

e) $(2 + 2) \times 3 = (2 \times 3) + (2 \times 3)$ _____

f) $3 \times (2 \times 7) = (3 \times 2) \times 7$ _____

g) $274 \times 35 = 35 \times 274$ _____

h) $(5 + 5) \times 5 = (5 \times 5) + (5 \times 5)$ _____

NS6-44 Powers

Remember: Multiplication is a short form for repeated addition: $5 \times 3 = 3 + 3 + 3 + 3 + 3$

Add five 3s

A **power** is a short form for repeated multiplication: $3^5 = 3 \times 3 \times 3 \times 3 \times 3$

Multiply five 3s

The **exponent** in a power tells you how many times to write the **base** in the product.

base $\longrightarrow 3^5 \longleftarrow$ exponent

1. Write the exponent and base for the power.

a) 2^3 base: __2__   b) 3^2 base: _____   c) 7^4 base: _____

       exponent: __3__   exponent: _____   exponent: _____

2. Write the power as a product.

a) $9^2 = 9 \times 9$ b) $7^3 =$ c) $8^4 =$

d) $2^3 =$ e) $1^4 =$ f) $0^3 =$

3. Write the product as a power.

a) $4 \times 4 \times 4 =$ b) $3 \times 3 \times 3 \times 3 =$ c) $8 \times 8 =$

d) $3 \times 3 \times 3 =$ e) $0 \times 0 \times 0 \times 0 \times 0 =$ **BONUS** ▶ $19 \times 19 \times 19 =$

REMINDER ▶ Multiplication is performed from left to right.

4. Evaluate the power. Keep track of the product as you go along.

a)

$3^5 = 3 \times 3 \times 3 \times 3 \times 3 =$ ☐

b)

$2^6 = 2 \times 2 \times 2 \times 2 \times 2 \times 2 =$ ☐

c)

$1^{10} = 1 \times 1 \times 1 \times 1 \times 1 \times 1 \times 1 \times 1 \times 1 \times 1 =$ ☐

d)

$10^5 = 10 \times 10 \times 10 \times 10 \times 10 =$

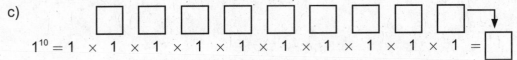
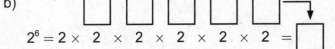
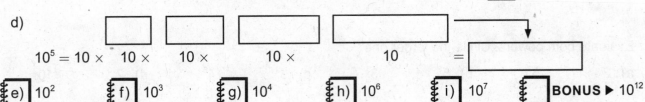

e) 10^2 f) 10^3 g) 10^4 h) 10^6 i) 10^7 **BONUS** ▶ 10^{12}

BONUS ▶ Predict: $1^{500} =$ _____

5. Evaluate the power first. Then multiply, divide, add, or subtract.

a) 5×2^2

$= 5 \times \underline{\quad 4 \quad}$

$= \underline{\quad 20 \quad}$

b) 3×2^3

$= 3 \times \underline{\qquad}$

$= \underline{\qquad}$

c) $4^2 + 4$

$= \underline{\qquad} + 4$

$= \underline{\qquad}$

d) $2 + 5^2$

$= 2 + \underline{\qquad}$

$= \underline{\qquad}$

e) 5×3^2

$= $

$= $

f) $10^2 \div 20$

$= $

$= $

g) $4^2 + 9$

$= $

$= $

h) $10 - 2^3$

$= $

$= $

When an expression involves powers, the correct order of operations is:

1. Do operations in brackets.
2. Evaluate powers.
3. Do multiplication and division, from left to right.
4. Do addition and subtraction, from left to right.

---

6. Which operation is done first? Do it, then rewrite the rest of the expression.

a) $4^2 - 5$

$= \underline{\quad 16 - 5 \quad}$

b) $2^5 \div 4$

$= \underline{\qquad}$

c) $4 \times 5 + 3^2$

$= \underline{\qquad}$

d) $18 \times 2 \div 3^2$

$= \underline{\qquad}$

7. Do the operations one at a time, in the correct order.

a) 5×2^3

b) $(5 \times 2)^3$

c) $5 + 2^3$

d) $(5 + 2)^3$

e) $(8 \div 2)^3$

f) $8 \div 2^3$

g) $(12 - 2)^3$

h) $12 - 2^3$

i) $24 \div 2^3$

j) $20 - 4^2 + 3$

k) $26^2 \div (3 + 1)$

l) $3 \times 2^2 + 4$

8. Evaluate both powers. Circle the larger one.

a) 2^5 5^2

$= \underline{\qquad}$ $= \underline{\qquad}$

b) 5^3 3^5

$= \underline{\qquad}$ $= \underline{\qquad}$

c) 3^4 4^3

$= \underline{\qquad}$ $= \underline{\qquad}$

d) 2^{10} 10^2

$= \underline{\qquad}$ $= \underline{\qquad}$

NS6-45 Division with Fractional Answers

Three people share 5 pancakes. How much does each person get?

Divide each pancake into thirds. Give each person one piece from each pancake.
The shaded parts show how much one person gets.

Each person gets $\frac{1}{3} + \frac{1}{3} + \frac{1}{3} + \frac{1}{3} + \frac{1}{3} = 5 \times \frac{1}{3} = \frac{5}{3}$ of a pancake.

1. Shade one person's share of the pancakes. How much does each person get?

   a) 4 people share 5 pancakes.

   _____ × _____ = _____ pancakes

   b) 2 people share 3 pancakes.

   _____ × _____ = _____ pancakes

2. Draw a picture to solve the problem.
   Four people share 9 oranges. How many oranges does each person get? _____

The division sign ($\div$) can be used for equal sharing, even when the answer is a fraction.

Example: When 3 people share 5 pancakes equally, each person gets $\frac{5}{3}$ of a pancake. So, $5 \div 3 = \frac{5}{3}$.

---

3. Draw a picture to show how much one person gets. Write the division equation.

   a) Two people share 9 objects.

   _____ $\div$ _____ = _____

   b) Three people share 8 objects.

   _____ $\div$ _____ = _____

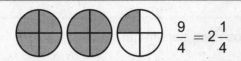

$$\frac{9}{4} = 2\frac{1}{4}$$

4. Divide. Write your answer as both an improper fraction and a mixed number.

   a) $8 \div 5 = \dfrac{8}{5} = 1\dfrac{3}{5}$

   b) $13 \div 4 =$

   c) $17 \div 5 =$

   d) $37 \div 10 =$

   e) $45 \div 8 =$

   f) $36 \div 5 =$

When dividing, you can divide the remainder separately.
Example: 4 people share 11 pies.

Start by giving each person 2 pies. Then divide the leftovers.

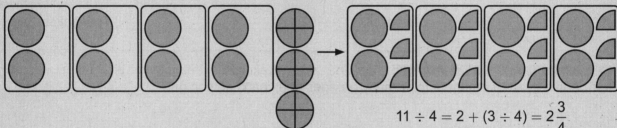

$$11 \div 4 = 2 + (3 \div 4) = 2\frac{3}{4}$$

Each person gets $2\dfrac{3}{4}$ pies.

5. Divide the remainder to write your answer as a mixed number.

   a) 3 people share 14 granola bars.

   Each person gets __4__ bars with __2__ left over.

   Now divide the leftovers too. $14 \div 3 = \boxed{4\dfrac{2}{3}}$

   b) 5 people share 14 pounds of rice.

   Each person gets ____ lb with ____ left over.

   Now divide the leftovers too. $14 \div 5 = \boxed{}$

   c) 5 people share 13 fruits.

   Each person gets ____ fruits with ____ left over.

   Now divide the leftovers too. $13 \div 5 = \boxed{}$

   d) 6 people share 50 pears.

   Each person gets ____ pears with ____ left over.

   Now divide the leftovers too. $50 \div 6 = \boxed{}$

6. Six people share a 50 lb bag of flour. How much flour does each person get?

7. A recipe for 6 muffins calls for 20 tablespoons of flour.
   How much flour is in each muffin?

NS6-46 Division, Fractions, and Decimals

> **REMINDER** ▶ You can write tenths, hundredths, and thousandths as decimals. The number of digits after the decimal point is equal to the number of zeros in the denominator.
>
> Examples: $\dfrac{7}{10} = 0.7$ $\dfrac{382}{100} = 3.82$ $\dfrac{17}{1,000} = 0.017$

1. Divide. Write the answer as a fraction and a decimal.

   a) $3 \div 10$

   $= \dfrac{3}{10}$

   $= 0.3$

   b) $28 \div 100$

   $=$

   $=$

   c) $43 \div 10$

   $=$

   $=$

   d) $8 \div 1,000$

   $=$

   $=$

   e) $542 \div 10$

   $=$

   $=$

   f) $863 \div 100$

   $=$

   $=$

   g) $94 \div 1,000$

   $=$

   $=$

   h) $80,403 \div 1,000$

   $=$

   $=$

> **REMINDER** ▶ You can change a fraction to a decimal by making the denominator equal to a power of 10. The powers of 10 are 10, 100, 1,000, ….
>
> Examples: $\dfrac{5}{4} = \dfrac{5 \times 25}{4 \times 25} = \dfrac{125}{100} = 1.25$

2. Divide. Write your answer as a decimal.

   a) $3 \div 5$

   $\dfrac{3}{5} = \dfrac{\boxed{}}{10} = \underline{}$

   b) $9 \div 5$

   $\dfrac{9}{5} = \dfrac{\boxed{}}{10} = \underline{}$

   c) $7 \div 20$

   $\dfrac{7}{20} = \dfrac{\boxed{}}{100} = \underline{}$

   d) $10 \div 4$

   e) $3 \div 4$

   f) $5 \div 2$

   g) $33 \div 20$

   BONUS ▶ $11 \div 8$

3. Compare your answers to parts d) and f). What do you notice? Why is that the case?

Here is $\frac{1}{3}$ of a rectangle.

Here is $\frac{1}{4}$ of $\frac{1}{3}$ of the rectangle.

How much is $\frac{1}{4}$ of $\frac{1}{3}$?

Expand the lines to find out.

$\frac{1}{4}$ of $\frac{1}{3} = \frac{1}{12}$

1. Extend the horizontal lines in the figure, and then write a fraction equation for the figure using the word "of."

a)

$\frac{1}{2}$ of $\frac{1}{4} = \frac{1}{8}$

b)

$\frac{1}{3}$ of $\frac{1}{5} =$

c)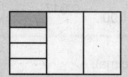

$\frac{1}{5}$ of $\frac{1}{2} =$

d)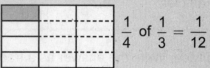

REMINDER ▶ The word "of" can mean "multiply."

2. Rewrite the fraction equations from Question 1 using the multiplication sign instead of the word "of."

a) $\frac{1}{2} \times \frac{1}{4} = \frac{1}{8}$ b)   c)   d)

3. Write a multiplication equation for the figure.

a)

$\frac{1}{3} \times \frac{1}{4} = \frac{1}{12}$

b)

c)

d)

$\frac{1}{3} \times \frac{1}{5} = \frac{1}{15} \longleftarrow 3 \times 5$

4. Multiply.

a) $\frac{1}{2} \times \frac{1}{7} =$ b) $\frac{1}{5} \times \frac{1}{6} =$ c) $\frac{1}{4} \times \frac{1}{6} =$ d) $\frac{1}{5} \times \frac{1}{4} =$

e) $\frac{1}{3} \times \frac{1}{2} =$ f) $\frac{1}{7} \times \frac{1}{4} =$ g) $\frac{1}{6} \times \frac{1}{5} =$ h) $\frac{1}{4} \times \frac{1}{4} =$

5. Circle two answers in Question 4 that are the same. How could you have predicted this?

| Here is $\frac{2}{3}$ of a rectangle. 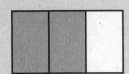 | Here is $\frac{4}{5}$ of $\frac{2}{3}$ of the rectangle. 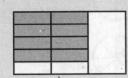 | How much is $\frac{4}{5}$ of $\frac{2}{3}$? Expand the lines to find out.  $\frac{4}{5}$ of $\frac{2}{3} = \frac{8}{15}$ |

6. Write a fraction equation for the figure. Use the multiplication sign instead of the word "of."

a)

b)

c)

d)

$$\frac{2}{7} \times \frac{3}{4} = \frac{6}{28}$$

$$\frac{5}{7} \times \frac{2}{3} =$$

$$\frac{4}{5} \times \frac{2}{3} = \frac{4 \times 2}{5 \times 3} = \frac{8}{15}$$

7. Multiply.

a) $\frac{2}{3} \times \frac{4}{7} = \frac{8}{21}$

b) $\frac{1}{2} \times \frac{3}{5} =$

c) $\frac{3}{4} \times \frac{5}{7} =$

d) $\frac{2}{3} \times \frac{10}{11} =$

e) $\frac{3}{4} \times \frac{3}{5} =$

f) $\frac{2}{5} \times \frac{4}{7} =$

BONUS ▶ $\frac{3}{2} \times \frac{3}{5} \times \frac{3}{7} =$

8. Ryan is making $\frac{1}{2}$ of a recipe for blueberry cobbler.

The recipe calls for $\frac{3}{4}$ of a cup of blueberries.

What fraction of a cup of blueberries does he need?

9. There was $\frac{3}{8}$ of a quiche left. Kira ate $\frac{3}{5}$ of it. What fraction of the whole quiche did Kira eat?

10. John spent $\frac{3}{5}$ of his free time playing outside. He spent $\frac{2}{3}$ of his outside time

playing soccer. What fraction of his free time did he spend playing soccer?

You can multiply improper fractions the same way you multiply proper fractions.

$\frac{5}{2} =$

$\frac{3}{4} \times \frac{5}{2} =$ $= \frac{15}{8}$

← 5 groups of 3 are shaded

← 2 groups of 4 in each whole

11. Multiply. Reduce your answers to lowest terms.

a) $\frac{2}{3} \times \frac{9}{5}$

b) $\frac{3}{4} \times \frac{12}{7}$

c) $\frac{1}{3} \times \frac{6}{5}$

d) $\frac{3}{2} \times \frac{8}{7}$

e) $\frac{3}{4} \times \frac{6}{5}$

f) $\frac{3}{5} \times \frac{7}{6}$

g) $\frac{8}{3} \times \frac{6}{5}$

h) $\frac{5}{4} \times \frac{9}{5}$

12. Change the mixed numbers to improper fractions and multiply. Write your answer as a mixed number.

a) $1\frac{1}{3} \times 1\frac{3}{5} = \frac{4}{3} \times \frac{8}{5}$

b) $2\frac{3}{4} \times 3\frac{1}{2} =$

$= \boxed{\frac{32}{15}}$ ← improper fraction

$= \boxed{2\frac{2}{15}}$ ← mixed number

$= \boxed{}$ ← improper fraction

$= \boxed{}$ ← mixed number

c) $3\frac{1}{3} \times 2\frac{7}{10}$

d) $1\frac{2}{3} \times 2\frac{1}{5}$

e) $2\frac{1}{4} \times 1\frac{2}{5}$

f) $2\frac{1}{3} \times 2\frac{2}{5}$

13. Lacey is making $\frac{3}{5}$ of a recipe for bread. The recipe calls for $3\frac{1}{2}$ cups of flour.

a) How much flour does she need? Hint: Change $3\frac{1}{2}$ to an improper fraction.

b) Lacey uses 2 cups of flour. Will her recipe turn out?

14. Louis is making $3\frac{1}{2}$ batches of dumplings. He needs $1\frac{3}{4}$ cups of flour for each batch.

a) How many cups of flour does he need?

b) He has 6 cups of flour. If he uses all his flour, will the recipe turn out?

NS6-48 Multiplying Decimals by Decimals

1. Shade squares to show the amount. Find the product.

a) 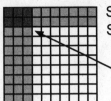 Shade 2 rows to show 2 tenths.
Shade 3 columns to show 3 tenths.

 $\dfrac{6}{100}$

$\dfrac{2}{10}$ of $\dfrac{3}{10}$ is $\dfrac{6}{100}$ so $\dfrac{2}{10} \times \dfrac{3}{10} = \dfrac{6}{100}$

b)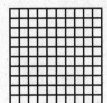

$\dfrac{2}{10} \times \dfrac{8}{10} =$

c)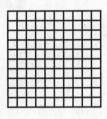

$\dfrac{7}{10} \times \dfrac{4}{10} =$

2. Write a multiplication equation for the figure.

a)

$\dfrac{7}{10} \times \dfrac{3}{10} = \dfrac{21}{100}$

b)

c)

d)

3. Multiply the fractions.

a) $\dfrac{3}{100} \times \dfrac{5}{10} = \dfrac{15}{1,000}$

b) $\dfrac{3}{10} \times \dfrac{5}{10} =$

c) $\dfrac{3}{100} \times \dfrac{5}{100} =$

d) $\dfrac{3}{1,000} \times \dfrac{5}{10} =$

e) $\dfrac{3}{1,000} \times \dfrac{5}{100} =$

f) $\dfrac{3}{100} \times \dfrac{5}{10,000} =$

4. Look at your answers to Question 3. How can you find the number of zeros in the denominator of the product before multiplying?

_____

_____

5. Multiply the fractions. Then write the fraction equation as a decimal equation.

a) $\dfrac{4}{10} \times \dfrac{2}{10} =$

$0.4 \times 0.2 =$

b) $\dfrac{3}{100} \times \dfrac{2}{100} =$

$0.03 \times 0.02 =$

c) $\dfrac{4}{10} \times \dfrac{3}{1,000} =$

d) $\dfrac{3}{100} \times \dfrac{9}{1,000} =$

6. Multiply the decimals as shown in part a).

a) $0.3 \times 0.7 = \dfrac{3}{10} \times \dfrac{7}{10} = \dfrac{21}{100} = 0.21$ b) $0.5 \times 0.4 =$

c) $0.2 \times 0.8 =$ d) $0.05 \times 0.4 =$

e) $0.05 \times 0.03 =$ f) $0.02 \times 0.007 =$

To multiply decimals, follow these steps.

Example:	**Step 1**	**Step 2**
13.5×0.08	Multiply the decimals as if they were whole numbers:	13.5 has **1 digit** after the decimal point and 0.08 has **2 digits** after the decimal point. Shift the decimal point $1 + 2 = 3$ places left:
	$135 \times 8 = 1{,}080$	1 0 8 0. So $13.5 \times 0.08 = 1.080$ or 1.08

---

7. Using the rule given above, multiply the decimals.

a) $0.2 \times 0.6 = \underline{\ 0.12\ }$

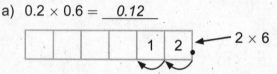
2×6

b) $0.5 \times 0.08 = \underline{\hspace{2cm}}$

5×8

c) $0.7 \times 0.9 = \underline{\hspace{2cm}}$

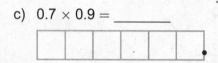

d) $0.005 \times 0.06 = \underline{\hspace{2cm}}$

e) $0.04 \times 0.67 = \underline{\hspace{2cm}}$

	6	7
$\times$		4

f) $4.5 \times 0.09 = \underline{\hspace{2cm}}$

$\times$		

g) 4.5×3.9 h) 6.8×0.73 **BONUS** ▶ $0.4 \times 0.003 \times 0.02 \times 0.02$

8. Stephanie bought 3.4 ounces of cheese. Each ounce of cheese costs $0.84. How much did she pay?

9. Find two numbers that multiply to 0.24. How many solutions can you find?

NS6-49 Dividing Fractions by Whole Numbers

Five people share $\frac{2}{3}$ of a cake. What fraction of the cake does each person get?

Divide $\frac{2}{3}$ among 5 equal groups. How much is in one group?

   so $\frac{2}{3} \div 5 = \frac{2}{15}$

1. Use the model to divide each fraction by 5.

a)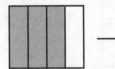

$\frac{3}{4} \div 5 = \frac{3}{20}$

b)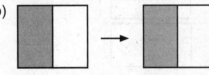

$\frac{1}{2} \div 5 =$

c)

$\frac{1}{3} \div 5 =$

d)

$\frac{3}{8} \div 5 =$

2. Finish the model to divide.

a)

$\frac{1}{2} \div 3 = \frac{1}{6}$

b)

$\frac{2}{3} \div 4 =$

c)

$\frac{2}{5} \div 3 =$

d)

$\frac{1}{4} \div 2 =$

3. Check your answers to Question 2 using multiplication. Example: Does $3 \times \frac{1}{6} = \frac{1}{2}$?

$$\frac{3}{5} \div 2 = \frac{3}{5 \times 2} = \frac{3}{10}$$

4. Divide. Check your answers using a picture.

a) $\frac{4}{5} \div 2 =$ b) $\frac{1}{4} \div 3 =$ c) $\frac{3}{4} \div 2 =$ d) $\frac{2}{3} \div 3 =$

5. Three people share $\frac{4}{5}$ of a lasagna equally. What fraction of a lasagna does each person eat?

6. Five people share $\frac{1}{2}$ of a pound of licorice equally. How much licorice does each person get?

NS6-50 Dividing Whole Numbers by Unit Fractions

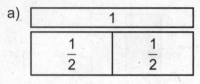

To divide $6 \div 2$, ask: How many 2s fit into 6?

| 2 | 2 | 2 |

So, $6 \div 2 = 3$

To divide $1 \div \dfrac{1}{3}$, ask: How many $\dfrac{1}{3}$s fit into 1?

| 1 | | |
| $\frac{1}{3}$ | $\frac{1}{3}$ | $\frac{1}{3}$ |

So, $1 \div \dfrac{1}{3} = 3$

1. How many fit into 1?

a)

| 1 | |
| $\frac{1}{2}$ | $\frac{1}{2}$ |

$1 \div \dfrac{1}{2} = $ _____

b)

| 1 | | | | |
| $\frac{1}{5}$ | $\frac{1}{5}$ | $\frac{1}{5}$ | $\frac{1}{5}$ | $\frac{1}{5}$ |

$1 \div \dfrac{1}{5} = $ _____

c) $1 \div \dfrac{1}{4} = $ _____   d) $1 \div \dfrac{1}{7} = $ _____

BONUS ▶ $1 \div \dfrac{1}{800,000} = $ _____

2. How many fit into 2?

a)

| 1 | | 1 | |
| $\frac{1}{2}$ | $\frac{1}{2}$ | $\frac{1}{2}$ | $\frac{1}{2}$ |

$2 \div \dfrac{1}{2} = $ _____

b)

| 1 | | | 1 | | |
| $\frac{1}{3}$ | $\frac{1}{3}$ | $\frac{1}{3}$ | $\frac{1}{3}$ | $\frac{1}{3}$ | $\frac{1}{3}$ |

$2 \div \dfrac{1}{3} = $ _____

c) $2 \div \dfrac{1}{5} = $ _____   d) $2 \div \dfrac{1}{10} = $ _____

BONUS ▶ $2 \div \dfrac{1}{1,000,000} = $ _____

3. Write the division equation the picture shows.

a)

| 1 | | 1 | | 1 | |
| $\frac{1}{2}$ | $\frac{1}{2}$ | $\frac{1}{2}$ | $\frac{1}{2}$ | $\frac{1}{2}$ | $\frac{1}{2}$ |

b)

| 1 | | | | 1 | | | |
| $\frac{1}{4}$ | $\frac{1}{4}$ | $\frac{1}{4}$ | $\frac{1}{4}$ | $\frac{1}{4}$ | $\frac{1}{4}$ | $\frac{1}{4}$ | $\frac{1}{4}$ |

_____   _____

c)

| 1 | | | | | 1 | | | | | 1 | | | | |
| $\frac{1}{5}$ | $\frac{1}{5}$ | $\frac{1}{5}$ | $\frac{1}{5}$ | $\frac{1}{5}$ | $\frac{1}{5}$ | $\frac{1}{5}$ | $\frac{1}{5}$ | $\frac{1}{5}$ | $\frac{1}{5}$ | $\frac{1}{5}$ | $\frac{1}{5}$ | $\frac{1}{5}$ | $\frac{1}{5}$ | $\frac{1}{5}$ |

_____

4. Use the number line to decide how many steps of size $\frac{1}{3}$ fit into 4.

```
|---|---|---|---|---|---|---|---|---|---|---|---|
0           1           2           3           4
```

Write the division equation. _____

5. Draw a number line to divide $4 \div \frac{1}{2}$.

6. There are 3 pizzas. Each slice is $\frac{1}{6}$ of a pizza. Write a division equation to show how many pieces there are.

_____

How many $\frac{1}{3}$s fit into 5? Three $\frac{1}{3}$s fit into 1, so 5 times as many fit into 5. $5 \div \frac{1}{3} = 5 \times 3 = 15$

---

7. Divide.

a) $3 \div \frac{1}{8} = $ _____ $\times$ _____

   $= $ _____

b) $5 \div \frac{1}{2} = $ _____ $\times$ _____

   $= $ _____

c) $4 \div \frac{1}{2} = $ _____

d) $2 \div \frac{1}{6} = $ _____

e) $3 \div \frac{1}{7} = $ _____

f) $8 \div \frac{1}{5} = $ _____

g) $8 \div \frac{1}{9} = $ _____

h) $7 \div \frac{1}{6} = $ _____

BONUS ▶ $3,000 \div \frac{1}{400} = $ _____

8. Farouk has 5 yards of ribbon to wrap gifts. He needs $\frac{1}{4}$ of a yard for each gift. How many gifts can he wrap?

9. Bilal only has a $\frac{1}{3}$ cup measuring spoon. He needs 4 cups of flour. How many spoonfuls does he need?

10. Karla has 3 submarine sandwiches. She cuts each sandwich into quarters.

a) How many pieces of sandwich does she have?

b) There are 6 people in her family. If she gives the same number of pieces to each person, how many does each person get?

1. How many $\dfrac{1}{6}$s fit into the shaded number?

a)

1

$\frac{1}{6}$	$\frac{1}{6}$	$\frac{1}{6}$	$\frac{1}{6}$	$\frac{1}{6}$	$\frac{1}{6}$

$1 \div \dfrac{1}{6} = $ _____

b)

1

$\frac{1}{2}$	$\frac{1}{2}$

$\frac{1}{6}$	$\frac{1}{6}$	$\frac{1}{6}$	$\frac{1}{6}$	$\frac{1}{6}$	$\frac{1}{6}$

$\dfrac{1}{2} \div \dfrac{1}{6} = $ _____

c)

1

$\frac{1}{3}$	$\frac{1}{3}$	$\frac{1}{3}$

$\frac{1}{6}$	$\frac{1}{6}$	$\frac{1}{6}$	$\frac{1}{6}$	$\frac{1}{6}$	$\frac{1}{6}$

$\dfrac{1}{3} \div \dfrac{1}{6} = $ _____

d)

1

$\frac{1}{3}$	$\frac{1}{3}$	$\frac{1}{3}$

$\frac{1}{6}$	$\frac{1}{6}$	$\frac{1}{6}$	$\frac{1}{6}$	$\frac{1}{6}$	$\frac{1}{6}$

$\dfrac{2}{3} \div \dfrac{1}{6} = $ _____

2. How many $\dfrac{1}{8}$s fit into the shaded number? Write the division equation.

a)

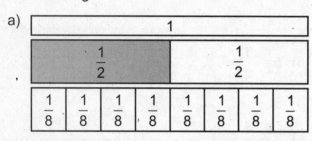

b)

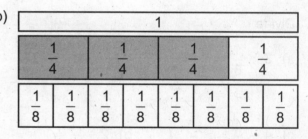

_____   _____

3. Divide the whole into tenths. How many $\dfrac{1}{10}$s fit into $\dfrac{4}{5}$? Write the division equation.

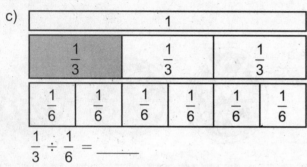

one whole

4. Draw a picture to divide $\dfrac{3}{5} \div \dfrac{1}{10}$.

Eight stamps make a strip that is 1 foot long.

Each stamp is $\frac{1}{8}$ of the strip.

$$1 \div \frac{1}{8} = 8$$

How many stamps fit into $\frac{3}{4}$ of the strip?

8 eighths fit into 1 strip.

So, $\frac{3}{4}$ of 8 eighths fit into $\frac{3}{4}$ of the strip.

$$\frac{3}{4} \div \frac{1}{8} = \frac{3}{4} \text{ of } 8 = \frac{3}{4} \times 8 = 6$$

5. Write the division as a multiplication.

a) $1 \div \frac{1}{6} = 6$

So, $\frac{2}{3} \div \frac{1}{6} = \frac{2}{3} \text{ of } 6 = \frac{2}{3} \times 6$

b) $1 \div \frac{3}{4} = $ _____

So, $\frac{3}{4} \div \frac{1}{12} = $

c) $1 \div \frac{1}{10} = $ _____

So, $\frac{3}{2} \div \frac{1}{10} = $

d) $1 \div \frac{1}{6} = $ _____

So, $\frac{5}{3} \div \frac{1}{6} = $

REMINDER ▶
$$\frac{3}{4} \times 8 = 8 \times \frac{3}{4} = \frac{8 \times 3}{4}$$
$$= \frac{24}{4}$$
$$= 6$$

---

6. Multiply the fraction and the whole number.

a) $\frac{3}{5} \times 10 = \frac{30}{5}$ ↙ 3×10

$= 6$

b) $\frac{2}{3} \times 6 = $

c) $\frac{3}{4} \times 12 = $

d) $\frac{2}{5} \times 20 = $

7. Use multiplication to divide.

a) $\frac{2}{3} \div \frac{1}{9} = \frac{2}{3} \times 9$

$= \frac{18}{3}$

$= 6$

b) $\frac{5}{4} \div \frac{1}{8} = $

c) $\frac{7}{3} \div \frac{1}{12} = $

d) $\frac{3}{2} \div \frac{1}{8} = $

8. Draw a picture to check your answer in Question 7b).

NS6-52 Dividing Whole Numbers by Fractions (Introduction)

1. Outline blocks of size $\frac{2}{5}$. How many fit into 2?

1					1				
$\frac{1}{5}$	$\frac{1}{5}$	$\frac{1}{5}$	$\frac{1}{5}$	$\frac{1}{5}$	$\frac{1}{5}$	$\frac{1}{5}$	$\frac{1}{5}$	$\frac{1}{5}$	$\frac{1}{5}$

$2 \div \frac{2}{5} = $ _____

2. Outline blocks of size $\frac{3}{4}$. How many fit into 6?

1				1				1				1				1				1			
$\frac{1}{4}$	$\frac{1}{4}$	$\frac{1}{4}$	$\frac{1}{4}$	$\frac{1}{4}$	$\frac{1}{4}$	$\frac{1}{4}$	$\frac{1}{4}$	$\frac{1}{4}$	$\frac{1}{4}$	$\frac{1}{4}$	$\frac{1}{4}$	$\frac{1}{4}$	$\frac{1}{4}$	$\frac{1}{4}$	$\frac{1}{4}$	$\frac{1}{4}$	$\frac{1}{4}$	$\frac{1}{4}$	$\frac{1}{4}$	$\frac{1}{4}$	$\frac{1}{4}$	$\frac{1}{4}$	$\frac{1}{4}$

$6 \div \frac{3}{4} = $ _____

3. Draw steps of size $\frac{2}{5}$ to decide how many fit into 4. Write the division equation.

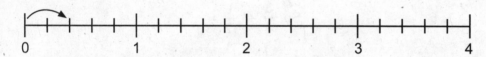

_____

4. a) A piece of ribbon is 4 m long. There are ___ *4 × 3* ___ pieces of size $\frac{1}{3}$ m in 4 m.

$\frac{2}{3}$ is 2 times as large as $\frac{1}{3}$, so only half as many will fit.

So, there are ___ *(4 × 3) ÷ 2* ___ pieces of size $\frac{2}{3}$ m in 4 m.

1			1			1			1		
$\frac{1}{3}$	$\frac{1}{3}$	$\frac{1}{3}$	$\frac{1}{3}$	$\frac{1}{3}$	$\frac{1}{3}$	$\frac{1}{3}$	$\frac{1}{3}$	$\frac{1}{3}$	$\frac{1}{3}$	$\frac{1}{3}$	$\frac{1}{3}$

b) A piece of ribbon is 6 m long. There are _____ pieces of size $\frac{1}{4}$ m in 6 m.

$\frac{3}{4}$ is 3 times as large as $\frac{1}{4}$, so only one third as many will fit.

So, there are _____ pieces of size $\frac{3}{4}$ m in 6 m.

1				1				1				1				1				1			
$\frac{1}{4}$	$\frac{1}{4}$	$\frac{1}{4}$	$\frac{1}{4}$	$\frac{1}{4}$	$\frac{1}{4}$	$\frac{1}{4}$	$\frac{1}{4}$	$\frac{1}{4}$	$\frac{1}{4}$	$\frac{1}{4}$	$\frac{1}{4}$	$\frac{1}{4}$	$\frac{1}{4}$	$\frac{1}{4}$	$\frac{1}{4}$	$\frac{1}{4}$	$\frac{1}{4}$	$\frac{1}{4}$	$\frac{1}{4}$	$\frac{1}{4}$	$\frac{1}{4}$	$\frac{1}{4}$	$\frac{1}{4}$

5. a) $10 \div \frac{2}{3} = $ ___ *(10 × 3) ÷ 2* ___   b) $8 \div \frac{4}{5} = $ _____   c) $9 \div \frac{3}{4} = $ _____

6. Divide.

a) $8 \div \frac{2}{3}$ b) $10 \div \frac{5}{6}$ c) $6 \div \frac{3}{8}$

NS6-53 Dividing 1 by a Fraction

1. Fill in the missing numbers.

a)

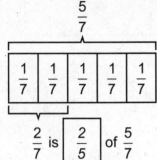

$$\frac{5}{7}$$

$$\frac{2}{7} \text{ is } \boxed{\frac{2}{5}} \text{ of } \frac{5}{7}$$

b)

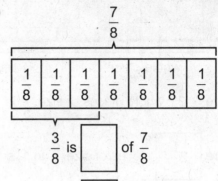

$$\frac{7}{8}$$

$$\frac{3}{8} \text{ is } \boxed{} \text{ of } \frac{7}{8}$$

c)

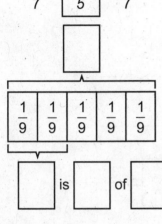

$$\boxed{} \text{ is } \boxed{} \text{ of } \boxed{}$$

d)

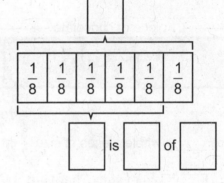

$$\boxed{} \text{ is } \boxed{} \text{ of } \boxed{}$$

2. Draw extra pieces to find the answer.

a)

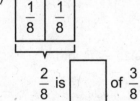

$$\frac{1}{5} \text{ is } \boxed{\frac{1}{3}} \text{ of } \frac{3}{5}$$

b)

$$\frac{3}{7} \text{ is } \boxed{} \text{ of } \frac{5}{7}$$

c)

$$\frac{2}{8} \text{ is } \boxed{} \text{ of } \frac{3}{8}$$

d)

$$\frac{3}{9} \text{ is } \boxed{} \text{ of } \frac{8}{9}$$

3. Fill in the missing numbers. Draw a picture in your notebook if it helps.

a) $\frac{4}{8}$ is $\boxed{}$ of $\frac{7}{8}$

b) $\frac{4}{9}$ is $\boxed{}$ of $\frac{7}{9}$

c) $\frac{4}{10}$ is $\boxed{}$ of $\frac{7}{10}$

d) $\frac{5}{9}$ is $\boxed{}$ of $\frac{8}{9}$

e) $\frac{2}{5}$ is $\boxed{}$ of $\frac{3}{5}$

f) $\frac{7}{100}$ is $\boxed{}$ of $\frac{9}{100}$

BONUS ▶ $\frac{8}{1,000,000}$ is $\boxed{}$ of $\frac{9}{1,000,000}$

4. What is the picture dividing by? Draw an extra piece of that size to divide.

a)

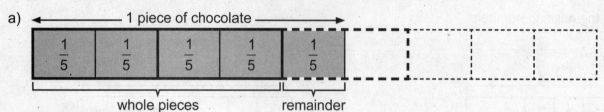

←————— 1 piece of chocolate —————→

| $\frac{1}{5}$ | $\frac{1}{5}$ | $\frac{1}{5}$ | $\frac{1}{5}$ | $\frac{1}{5}$ |

whole pieces   remainder

There are __2__ whole pieces of size $\frac{2}{5}$ in 1. The remainder is $\boxed{\frac{1}{2}}$ of $\frac{2}{5}$.

There are $\boxed{2\frac{1}{2}}$ pieces of size $\frac{2}{5}$ in 1, so $1 \div \frac{2}{5} = \boxed{2\frac{1}{2}}$.

b)

←————— 1 piece of chocolate —————→

| $\frac{1}{7}$ | $\frac{1}{7}$ | $\frac{1}{7}$ | $\frac{1}{7}$ | $\frac{1}{7}$ | $\frac{1}{7}$ | $\frac{1}{7}$ |

remainder

There are _____ whole pieces of size $\frac{3}{7}$ in 1. The remainder is $\boxed{}$ of $\frac{3}{7}$.

There are $\boxed{}$ pieces of size $\frac{3}{7}$ in 1, so $1 \div \frac{3}{7} = \boxed{}$.

c)

←————— 1 piece of chocolate —————→

| $\frac{1}{7}$ | $\frac{1}{7}$ | $\frac{1}{7}$ | $\frac{1}{7}$ | $\frac{1}{7}$ | $\frac{1}{7}$ | $\frac{1}{7}$ |

remainder

$1 \div \frac{2}{7} =$

5. Complete the picture to divide. Write your answer two ways.

a) How many blocks of size $\frac{3}{4}$ fit into 1?

←— 1 —→

| $\frac{1}{4}$ | $\frac{1}{4}$ | $\frac{1}{4}$ | $\frac{1}{4}$ |

$1 \div \frac{3}{4} = \boxed{}$ ←——— mixed number

$= \boxed{}$ ←——— improper fraction

b) How many blocks of size $\frac{2}{3}$ fit into 1?

←— 1 —→

| $\frac{1}{3}$ | $\frac{1}{3}$ | $\frac{1}{3}$ |

$1 \div \frac{2}{3} = \boxed{}$ ←——— mixed number

$= \boxed{}$ ←——— improper fraction

6.  Draw a picture to divide $1 \div \frac{2}{9}$. Write your answer two ways.

NS6-54 Dividing by Fractions

To divide 1 by a fraction, turn the fraction upside down! Example: $1 \div \dfrac{2}{5} = \dfrac{5}{2}$

Draw blocks of size $\dfrac{2}{5}$ to see how many fit into 1.

1

$\frac{1}{5}$	$\frac{1}{5}$	$\frac{1}{5}$	$\frac{1}{5}$	$\frac{1}{5}$	$\frac{1}{5}$

Each piece is $\dfrac{1}{2}$ of a block. There are 5 pieces in one whole. So, $\dfrac{5}{2}$ of a block fit into one whole.

1. Divide.

   a) $1 \div \dfrac{4}{5} =$

   b) $1 \div \dfrac{5}{8} =$

   c) $1 \div \dfrac{3}{5} =$

   BONUS ▶ Check your answer to part b) by drawing a picture.

REMINDER ▶ You can check division by using multiplication: Since $8 \div 2 = 4$, then $2 \times 4 = 8$.

2. Divide by turning the fraction upside down. Check your answer using multiplication.

   a) $1 \div \dfrac{8}{3} = \dfrac{3}{8}$

   b) $1 \div \dfrac{7}{5} =$

   c) $1 \div \dfrac{5}{9} =$

   Check: $\dfrac{8}{3} \times \dfrac{3}{8} = \dfrac{24}{24} = \boldsymbol{1} \checkmark$ Check: Check:

3. Divide using the picture.

   a) $1 \div \dfrac{2}{3} =$ _____

1

$\frac{1}{3}$	$\frac{1}{3}$	$\frac{1}{3}$	$\frac{1}{3}$

   b) $2 \div \dfrac{2}{3} =$ _____

1	1

$\frac{1}{3}$	$\frac{1}{3}$	$\frac{1}{3}$	$\frac{1}{3}$	$\frac{1}{3}$	$\frac{1}{3}$

   c) $3 \div \dfrac{2}{3} =$ _____

1	1	1

$\frac{1}{3}$	$\frac{1}{3}$	$\frac{1}{3}$	$\frac{1}{3}$	$\frac{1}{3}$	$\frac{1}{3}$	$\frac{1}{3}$	$\frac{1}{3}$	$\frac{1}{3}$	$\frac{1}{3}$

   d) Predict: $4 \div \dfrac{2}{3} =$ _____

4. How many $\dfrac{3}{8}$-cup servings are in 1 cup of cottage cheese? Between what two whole numbers does your answer lie?

5. A rectangular field with area 1 square mile is $\dfrac{3}{5}$ of a mile wide. How long is it?

To divide $4 \div \dfrac{2}{3}$, ask: How many $\dfrac{2}{3}$s fit into 4?

Four times as many as fit into 1.

$1 \div \dfrac{2}{3} = \dfrac{3}{2}$ so $4 \div \dfrac{2}{3} = 4 \times \dfrac{3}{2}$

$= \dfrac{12}{2}$

$= 6$

6. Write the division as a multiplication. Then divide.

a) $8 \div \dfrac{3}{4} = 8 \times \boxed{}$

b) $3 \div \dfrac{4}{7} = 3 \times \boxed{}$

c) $6 \div \dfrac{3}{5} = 6 \times \boxed{}$

d) $2 \div \dfrac{3}{8} =$

e) $4 \div \dfrac{2}{5} =$

f) $3 \div \dfrac{5}{8} =$

g) $12 \div \dfrac{4}{5} =$

h) $3 \div \dfrac{3}{5} =$

i) $9 \div \dfrac{3}{2} =$

To divide $\dfrac{4}{5} \div \dfrac{2}{3}$, ask: How many $\dfrac{2}{3}$s fit into $\dfrac{4}{5}$?

Four fifths as many as fit into 1.

$1 \div \dfrac{2}{3} = \dfrac{3}{2}$ so $\dfrac{4}{5} \div \dfrac{2}{3} = \dfrac{4}{5} \times \dfrac{3}{2}$

$= \dfrac{12}{10}$

$= \dfrac{6}{5}$

7. Write the division as a multiplication.

a) $\dfrac{2}{5} \div \dfrac{3}{8} = \dfrac{2}{5} \times \boxed{}$

b) $\dfrac{3}{8} \div \dfrac{2}{7} = \dfrac{3}{8} \times \boxed{}$

c) $\dfrac{4}{9} \div \dfrac{2}{3} = \dfrac{4}{9} \times \boxed{}$

REMINDER ▶ $\dfrac{2}{5} \times \dfrac{3}{7} = \dfrac{2 \times 3}{5 \times 7} = \dfrac{6}{35}$

8. Divide.

a) $\dfrac{3}{4} \div \dfrac{5}{2} = \dfrac{3}{4} \times \dfrac{2}{5}$

$\quad = \dfrac{6}{20}$

$\quad = \dfrac{3}{10}$

b) $\dfrac{7}{10} \div \dfrac{2}{3} =$

c) $\dfrac{3}{4} \div \dfrac{3}{5} =$

9. Check your answers to Question 8 using multiplication.

a) $\dfrac{5}{2} \times \dfrac{3}{10} = \dfrac{15}{20}$

$\quad = \dfrac{3}{4}$

b)

c)

10. Divide. Hint: Convert the mixed numbers to improper fractions.

a) $4\dfrac{2}{3} \div \dfrac{3}{5} = \dfrac{14}{3} \times \dfrac{5}{3}$

$\quad = \dfrac{70}{9} = 7\dfrac{7}{9}$

b) $1\dfrac{3}{4} \div \dfrac{3}{4} =$

c) $\dfrac{3}{4} \div 1\dfrac{1}{2} =$

d) $3\dfrac{1}{2} \div 2\dfrac{1}{3} =$

e) $1\dfrac{5}{7} \div 1\dfrac{1}{3} =$

f) $2\dfrac{1}{2} \div 3\dfrac{1}{3} =$

11. How many $\dfrac{2}{3}$-cup servings are in $\dfrac{4}{5}$ of a cup of yogurt?

12. How wide is a rectangular strip of land with length $1\dfrac{7}{8}$ miles and area $\dfrac{3}{4}$ square miles?

13. Aiden needs $2\dfrac{1}{2}$ cups of flour for a Danish strudel recipe. He only has a $\dfrac{2}{3}$-cup measuring spoon. How many spoonfuls does he need?

NS6-55 Word Problems (Advanced)

1. Rasheed has $\frac{7}{5}$ cups of flour. He used $\frac{3}{4}$ of the flour to bake a pie.

   a) How much flour did he use?

   b) Did Rasheed use more or less than a cup of flour? How do you know?

2. Sam biked $\frac{2}{3}$ km in 4 minutes. How far did he bike in 1 minute?

3. Dimitra ran 2.4 km each hour for 3 hours. How far did she run?

4. A string of length $3\frac{1}{2}$ m is divided into 5 equal pieces. How long is each piece?

5. A fruit flan recipe calls for $1\frac{1}{3}$ cups strawberry jam. The fruit flan is divided into 8 pieces.

   How much jam is in each piece?

6. Rosa is having a pasta party. She has $\frac{7}{4}$ lb of dry spaghetti.

   Each person needs $\frac{3}{16}$ lb. How many people can she feed?

7. How many months old is a $1\frac{1}{2}$-year-old child?

8. A string of length $4\frac{4}{5}$ m is divided into pieces of length $\frac{3}{10}$ m.

   How many pieces are there?

9. The price of a soccer ball is $8.00. If the price rises by $0.25 each year, how much will the ball cost in 10 years?

NS6-56 Fractions and Order of Operations (Advanced)

1. Evaluate these expressions. Do the operation in brackets first.

   a) $\dfrac{2}{5} + \left(\dfrac{1}{5} \times 4\right)$

   b) $\left(\dfrac{2}{5} + \dfrac{1}{5}\right) \times 4$

   c) $\dfrac{1}{3} + \left(\dfrac{4}{3} \div 2\right)$

   d) $\left(\dfrac{1}{3} + \dfrac{4}{3}\right) \div 2$

   e) $\dfrac{4}{3} - \left(\dfrac{2}{3} \times 2\right)$

   f) $\left(\dfrac{4}{3} - \dfrac{2}{3}\right) \times 2$

2. Compare the problems that are similar in Question 1. Does the order you do the

   operations in affect the answer? _____

REMINDER ▶ Mathematicians have ordered the operations to avoid writing brackets all the time.

Do operations in this order:
   1. Operations in brackets
   2. Multiplication and division, from left to right
   3. Addition and subtraction, from left to right

Examples: $7 - 5 \times \dfrac{2}{5} + 4 = 7 - 2 + 4$ but $(7 - 5) \times \left(\dfrac{2}{5} + 4\right) = 2 \times \dfrac{22}{5}$

$\qquad\qquad\qquad\qquad = 5 + 4 \qquad\qquad\qquad\qquad\qquad = \dfrac{44}{5}$

$\qquad\qquad\qquad\qquad = 9 \qquad\qquad\qquad\qquad\qquad\quad = 8\dfrac{4}{5}$

---

3. Which operation is done first? Do it, and then rewrite the rest of the expression.

   a) $\left(\dfrac{2}{3} + \dfrac{1}{2}\right) \times \dfrac{1}{4}$

   b) $\dfrac{2}{3} + \dfrac{1}{2} \times \dfrac{1}{4}$

   c) $\dfrac{3}{2} \div \left(\dfrac{5}{6} - \dfrac{1}{2}\right)$

   $= \left(\dfrac{4}{6} + \dfrac{3}{6}\right) \times \dfrac{1}{4}$

   $= \dfrac{7}{6} \times \dfrac{1}{4}$

4. Evaluate.

   a) $\dfrac{2}{3} \div \dfrac{1}{4} + \dfrac{1}{2}$

   b) $\dfrac{2}{3} \div \left(\dfrac{1}{4} + \dfrac{1}{2}\right)$

   c) $\dfrac{2}{3} - \dfrac{1}{4} \times \dfrac{1}{2}$

REMINDER ▶ Repeated multiplication is written as a power.

Examples: $3^4 = 3 \times 3 \times 3 \times 3$ and $\left(\dfrac{2}{3}\right)^4 = \dfrac{2}{3} \times \dfrac{2}{3} \times \dfrac{2}{3} \times \dfrac{2}{3} = \dfrac{2 \times 2 \times 2 \times 2}{3 \times 3 \times 3 \times 3} = \dfrac{16}{81}$

5. Write the power as a product.

a) $\left(\dfrac{1}{2}\right)^3 = \dfrac{1}{2} \times \dfrac{1}{2} \times \dfrac{1}{2}$ b) $\left(\dfrac{2}{5}\right)^4 =$ c) $\left(\dfrac{3}{4}\right)^5 =$

6. Evaluate the power.

a) $\left(\dfrac{1}{4}\right)^3 =$ b) $\left(\dfrac{3}{2}\right)^3 =$ c) $\left(\dfrac{2}{3}\right)^4 =$

REMINDER ▶ The correct order of operations is:

1. Operations in brackets
2. Powers
3. Multiplication and division, from left to right
4. Addition and subtraction, from left to right

7. Evaluate the expressions.

a) $\left(1 + \dfrac{2}{3}\right)^2$ b) $1 + \left(\dfrac{2}{3}\right)^2$ c) $\left(1 - \dfrac{2}{3}\right)^2$

d) $1 - \left(\dfrac{2}{3}\right)^2$ e) $\left(\dfrac{3}{10} \times 5\right)^2$ f) $\dfrac{3}{10} \div 5^2$

g) $\left(\dfrac{3}{10}\right)^2 \times 5$ h) $\left(\dfrac{1}{5} \div 2\right)^3$ i) $\dfrac{1}{5} \div 2^3$

REMINDER ▶ To multiply decimals, multiply the whole numbers and then shift the decimal point the total number of places it is shifted.

Example: $12 \times 12 = 144$ so $1.2 \times 1.2 = 1.44$

8. a) Evaluate $0.4^2 = 0.4 \times 0.4$.

b) Evaluate $\left(\dfrac{2}{5}\right)^2$. Change your answer to a decimal.

c) Compare your answers to parts a) and b). What do you notice? Why is this the case?

NS6-57 Dividing Decimals by Whole Numbers

> **REMINDER ▶** To divide by 10, 100, or 1,000, move the decimal point 1, 2, or 3 places left.
>
> Example: 85 = 85.0, so
>
> $85 ÷ 10 = 8.5$ $85 ÷ 100 = 0.85$ $85 ÷ 1,000 = 0.085$

1. Divide.

a) $3 ÷ 100 = $ _____

b) $43 ÷ 10 = $ _____

c) $62 ÷ 100 = $ _____

d) $485 ÷ 1,000 = $ _____

e) $485 ÷ 100 = $ _____

f) $485 ÷ 10 = $ _____

2. Count how many places you would shift the decimal point to make a whole number. Then write a division statement.

a)

	0	.	0	6

__2__ places   two zeros

$0.06 = 6 ÷ $ __100__

b)

0	.	0	7	6

_____ places

$0.076 = 76 ÷ $ _____

c)

		5	4	.	3

_____ places

$54.3 = 543 ÷ $ _____

d)

0	.	8	7	4

$0.874 = $ _____

e)

0	.	0	5	

$0.05 = $ _____

f)

2	.	5	7	

$2.57 = $ _____

3. Rewrite the division statement so that you are dividing a whole number by 10 or 100.

a) $3.2 ÷ 4$

$= (\underline{32} ÷ \underline{10}) ÷ \underline{4}$

$= (\underline{32} ÷ \underline{4}) ÷ \underline{10}$

b) $0.25 ÷ 5$

$= (\underline{\hspace{1cm}} ÷ \underline{\hspace{1cm}}) ÷ \underline{\hspace{1cm}}$

$= (\underline{\hspace{1cm}} ÷ \underline{\hspace{1cm}}) ÷ \underline{\hspace{1cm}}$

c) $0.12 ÷ 3$

$= $ _____

$= $ _____

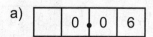 d) $4.5 ÷ 9$

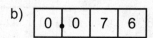 e) $0.06 ÷ 2$

 f) $3.06 ÷ 3$

4. Rewrite the division statement in one step, and then divide.

a) $2.4 ÷ 6$

$= \underline{(24 ÷ 6) ÷ 10}$

$= \underline{4 ÷ 10 = 0.4}$

b) $0.35 ÷ 5$

$= $ _____

$= $ _____

c) $0.042 ÷ 6$

$= $ _____

$= $ _____

d) $3.2 ÷ 8$

e) $4.26 ÷ 2$

f) $0.009 ÷ 3$

5. Karen cycles 0.24 miles in 8 minutes. How far does she cycle in 1 minute?

To divide 5.12 ÷ 2 using long division:

Step 1: Divide as though they are whole numbers.

Step 2: Put the decimal point in the quotient directly above the decimal point in the dividend.

```
      2  5  6              2. 5  6
   2) 5  1  2           2) 5. 1  2
     -4  ↓  ↓             -4
      1  1                 1  1
     -1  0  ↓    →        -1  0
         1  2                1  2
        -1  2               -1  2
            0                   0
```

So, 5.12 ÷ 2 = 2.56.

6. Place the decimal point in the correct place. Add any zeros you need to.

a)
```
    1  4  6
 3) 4 . 3  8
```

b)
```
    1  4  6
 3) 4  3 . 8
```

c)
```
       1  4  6
 3) 0 . 4  3  8
```

d)
```
    1  4  6
 3) 4  3  8  0 .
```

7. Divide as though the decimal numbers are whole numbers. Then put the decimal point in the correct place.

a)
```
    1 .
 3) 4 . 3  2
```

b)
```
 4) 6  2 . 8
```

c)
```
 5) 6  2 . 5
```

d)
```
 2) 3  3 . 2
```

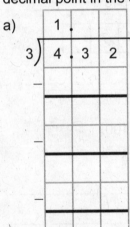

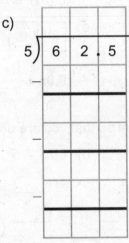

e) 8)1.44   f) 7)9.1   g) 8)2.72   h) 5)20.5

8. Five apples cost $2.75. How much does each apple cost?

9. Dita cycled 62.4 km in 4 hours. How many kilometers did she cycle in an hour?

10. Four friends earn a total of $29.16 shovelling snow. How much does each friend earn?

11. In a four-person relay, a team finished in 56.4 seconds. What was the average running time for each person?

12. Which is a better deal: 6 pens for $4.98 or 8 pens for $6.96?

NS6-58 Dividing by Decimals

1. a) Show how many 2s fit into 8.

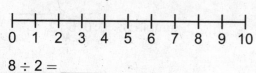

$8 \div 2 =$ _____

b) Show how many 0.2s fit into 0.8.

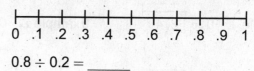

$0.8 \div 0.2 =$ _____

2. a) Show how many 3s fit into 6.

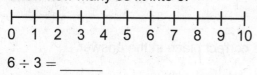

$6 \div 3 =$ _____

b) Show how many 0.3s fit into 0.6.

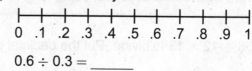

$0.6 \div 0.3 =$ _____

3. Write a whole number division that has the same answer. Then divide.

a) $0.6 \div 0.2$

= _____6 ÷ 2_____

= _____

b) $0.9 \div 0.3$

= _____

= _____

c) $0.8 \div 0.4$

= _____

= _____

d) $1 \div 0.2$

= _____

= _____

REMINDER ▶ To multiply a whole number by 10, add a zero.
To multiply a decimal by 10, move the decimal point one place to the right.

Examples: $23 \times 10 = 230$ $2.04 \times 10 = 20.4$

---

4. Multiply by 10.

a) $34 \times 10 =$ ___340___   b) $0.07 \times 10 =$ _____   c) $0.85 \times 10 =$ _____   d) $2.7 \times 10 =$ _____

To divide $1.4 \div 0.2$, multiply both numbers by 10:

$$1.4 \div 0.2 = (1.4 \times 10) \div (0.2 \times 10)$$
$$= 14 \div 2$$
$$= 7$$

---

5. Multiply both numbers by 10 or 100 to make the **divisor** a whole number. Then divide.

a) $0.12 \div 0.4 \overset{\text{divisor}}{\longleftarrow}$

_____$1.2 \div 4 = 0.3$_____

b) $1.6 \div 0.2$

_____

c) $28 \div 0.7$

_____

d) $0.36 \div 0.9$

_____

e) $24 \div 0.06$

= ___$2,400 \div 6$___

= _____400_____

f) $35 \div 0.05$

= _____

= _____

g) $0.3 \div 0.02$

= _____

= _____

h) $1.8 \div 0.03$

= _____

= _____

To divide by a decimal, make the divisor a whole number: Multiply both the dividend and the divisor by the same power of 10.

Example 1: $0.6\overline{)2.4}$ Example 2: $0.6\overline{)0.2\,4}$ Example 3: $0.06\overline{)2\,4.}$

$\longrightarrow 6\overline{)2\,4.}$ $\longrightarrow 6\overline{)2.4}$ $\longrightarrow 6\overline{)2\,4\,0\,0.}$

Then divide by the whole number using long division.

6. Use $156 \div 12 = 13$ to divide. Put the decimal point in the correct place in the answer.

a)
$$1.2\overline{)1\,5.6}\quad 1\,3$$

b)
$$1.2\overline{)1.5\,6}\quad 1\,3$$

c)
$$0.1\,2\overline{)1.5\,6}\quad 1\,3$$

You may need to add zeros.

d)
$$0.12\overline{)1\,5.6\,0}\quad 1\,3\,0$$

e)
$$1.2\overline{)1\,5\,6}\quad 1\,3$$

f)
$$0.0\,1\,2\overline{)1\,5.6}\quad 1\,3$$

BONUS▶ $0 . 0 \quad 0 \quad 0 \quad 0 \quad 1 \quad 2\overline{)1\,.\,5\,6}$

		1	3						

7. Use long division to divide.

a) $0.8\overline{)2.5\,6}$ $8\overline{)2\ 5\ .\ 6}$

b) $0.09\overline{)3\,1.5}$ 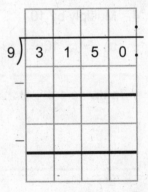 $9\overline{)3\ 1\ 5\ 0\ .}$

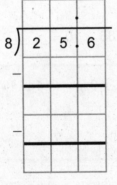

c) $16.74 \div 0.03$ d) $0.176 \div 0.08$ e) $13.47 \div 0.002$ f) $86.52 \div 0.4$

8. Evaluate each expression. Use the correct order of operations.

a) $4.8 \div (0.2 + 0.4)$ b) $4.8 \div 0.2 + 0.4$ c) $3.2 + 4.8 \times 5$ d) $(3.2 + 4.8) \times 5$

9. Carmela has 3.6 pounds of cheese. She needs 0.05 pounds of cheese for each sandwich. How many sandwiches can she make?

10. Elias has $3.52. How many $0.08 beads can he buy?

NS6-59 2-Digit Division (Introduction)

1. Circle the number of tens in the number being divided.

a) 11)(3 8)4

   There are 38 tens in 384.

b) 11)5 9 3

c) 11)6 3 2

2. How many times does 11 divide into the number of tens? Write your answer above the tens digit.

a)

	3	
11) | 3 | 8 | 4 |

b)

11) | 5 | 9 | 3 |

c)

11) | 6 | 3 | 2 |

d)

11) | 9 | 1 | 3 |

e)

11) | 7 | 5 | 3 |

f)

11) | 5 | 1 | 2 |

3. How many times does 21 divide into the number of tens? Write 0, 1, 2, 3, or 4.

a)

21) | 6 | 5 | 2 |

b)

21) | 4 | 9 | 6 |

c)

21) | 7 | 0 | 5 |

d)

21) | 9 | 2 | 0 |

e)

21) | 1 | 9 | 8 |

f)

21) | 2 | 1 | 6 |

4. Circle the first part of the number being divided that is at least 18.

   Is 3 at least 18? No. Is 37 at least 18? Yes.

a) 18)(37)2

b) 18)1 4 7

c) 18)1 8 5

d) 18)9 3 2

e) 18)4 7 6

f) 18)1 2 3

18	18	18	18	18	18	18	18	18
× 1	× 2	× 3	× 4	× 5	× 6	× 7	× 8	× 9
18	36	54	72	90	108	126	144	162

5. How many times does 18 divide into the circled number? Write your answer above the ones digit of the circled number.

a)

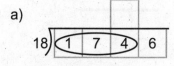

b)

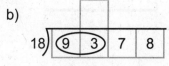

c)

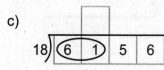

d)

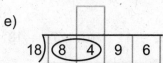

e)

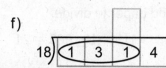

f)

18 people share $1,368. How much money does each person get?

Step 1: Break the money into 136 ten-dollar bills and 8 one-dollar bills.

Step 2: Divide the ten-dollar bills.

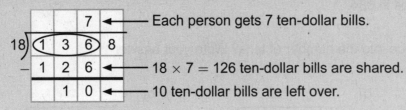

Each person gets 7 ten-dollar bills.

$18 \times 7 = 126$ ten-dollar bills are shared.

10 ten-dollar bills are left over.

6. Do the first two steps of long division.

a)
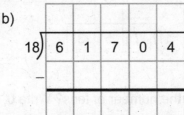

b)
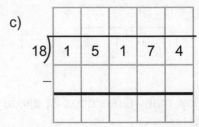

c)

Step 3: Trade the leftover ten-dollar bills for one-dollar bills and divide the remaining one-dollar bills.

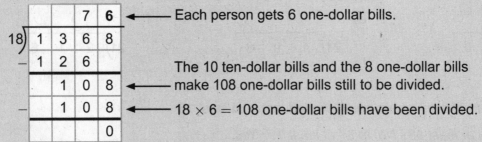

Each person gets 6 one-dollar bills.

The 10 ten-dollar bills and the 8 one-dollar bills make 108 one-dollar bills still to be divided.

$18 \times 6 = 108$ one-dollar bills have been divided.

$1,368 \div 18 = 76$, so each person gets $76.

7. Complete the long division.

a)
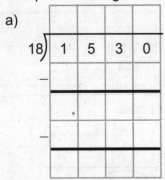

b)
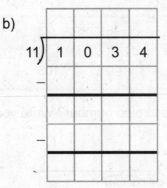

c)
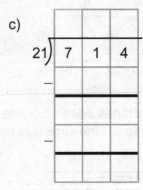

8. Use grid paper to divide.

a) $638 \div 11$ b) $903 \div 21$ c) $792 \div 11$ d) $774 \div 18$ e) $1638 \div 18$ f) $7092 \div 18$

NS6-60 2-Digit Division

When using long division, 237 ÷ 50 and 23 ÷ 5 have the same quotient but different remainders.
Since 5 × 4 = 20, then 50 × 4 = 200, and the answers are:

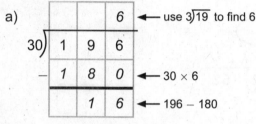 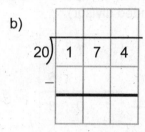 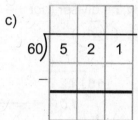

1. Divide by long division.

a) 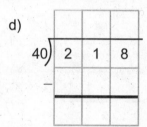 ← use 3)19 to find 6

30)1 9 6

− 1 8 0 ← 30 × 6

1 6 ← 196 − 180

b)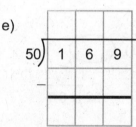

c)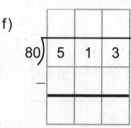

d)

e)

f)

g)

---

38 is close to 40, so 176 ÷ 38 is close to 176 ÷ 40.

2. Round the divisor to the nearest ten. Then estimate the quotient.

(50)   (   )   (   )   (   )

a) $\dfrac{3}{48)163}$ b) $69)478$ c) $32)235$ d) $41)333$

3. Multiply the divisor by the estimated quotient. Write the answer under the dividend.

a) $\dfrac{3}{48)162}$
   1 4 4

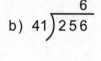

b) $\dfrac{6}{41)256}$

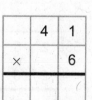

c) $\dfrac{7}{19)142}$

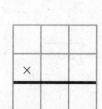

d) $\dfrac{8}{32)268}$

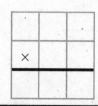

To divide 176 ÷ 38:

Step 1: Round the divisor → (40)
to the nearest ten.

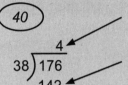

Step 2: Estimate the quotient
Use 176 ÷ 40 or 17 ÷ 4.

```
      4
38) 1 7 6
  − 1 4 2
      3 4
```

Step 3: Multiply the divisor by the
estimated quotient: 38 × 4 = 142.

Step 4: Subtract to find the remainder.

---

4. Round the divisor and estimate the quotient. Multiply the estimated quotient
by the divisor (*not* the rounded divisor).

a) (20)

```
        6
18) 1 2 2
    1 0 8
```

	1	8
×		6
1	0	8

b) ( )

```
42) 3 5 3
```

×		

c) ( )

```
49) 3 7 8
```

×		

d) ( )

```
32) 2 6 8
```

×		

5. Subtract to find the remainder.

a)
			4
62)	2	7	4
−	2	4	8
		2	6

b)
			6
29)	1	9	6
−	1	7	4

c)
		5	
41)	2	1	3
−	2	0	5

d)
			7
78)	5	9	4
−	5	4	6

6. Divide.

a) (60)

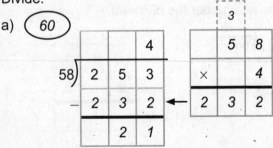

			4
58)	2	5	3
−	2	3	2
		2	1

```
      ⌐ 3 ⌐
    5 8
  ×     4
  2 3 2
```

b) ( )

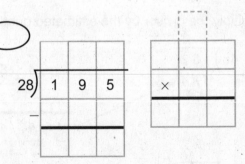

```
28) 1 9 5
  −
```

c) 19) 1 4 3   d) 32) 1 3 0   e) 49) 3 8 5   f) 21) 1 7 3

COPYRIGHT © 2013 JUMP MATH: NOT TO BE COPIED. CC EDITION

When estimating the quotient in a division problem, your estimate might be too high or too low.

Examples:

$$\begin{array}{r} 7 \\ 23\overline{)156} \\ -161 \\ \hline \end{array}$$
negative number!

TOO HIGH!

$$\begin{array}{r} 6 \\ 16\overline{)123} \\ -96 \\ \hline 27 \end{array}$$ but 27 > 16

TOO LOW!

1. Was the estimate too high or too low?

a) $\begin{array}{r} 6 \\ 18\overline{)135} \\ -108 \\ \hline \end{array}$

b) $\begin{array}{r} 6 \\ 23\overline{)135} \\ -138 \\ \hline \end{array}$

c) $\begin{array}{r} 9 \\ 43\overline{)362} \\ -387 \\ \hline \end{array}$

d) $\begin{array}{r} 4 \\ 27\overline{)149} \\ -108 \\ \hline \end{array}$

6 is too _____ .

6 is too _____ .

9 is too _____ .

4 is too _____ .

2. Use the first estimate to make a better estimate. Then divide.

a) $\begin{array}{r} 4 \\ 26\overline{)149} \\ -104 \\ \hline \mathbf{45} \end{array}$ 45 >26
TOO LOW!

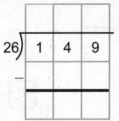

b) $\begin{array}{r} 6 \\ 17\overline{)135} \\ -102 \\ \hline \mathbf{33} \end{array}$ 33 >17
TOO LOW!

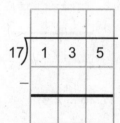

c) $\begin{array}{r} 6 \\ 17\overline{)121} \\ -102 \\ \hline \mathbf{19} \end{array}$ 19 >17
TOO LOW!

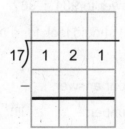

d) $\begin{array}{r} 6 \\ 23\overline{)129} \\ -138 \\ \hline \end{array}$
negative number!
TOO HIGH!

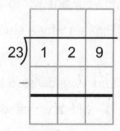

e) $\begin{array}{r} 8 \\ 34\overline{)263} \\ -272 \\ \hline \end{array}$
negative number!
TOO HIGH!

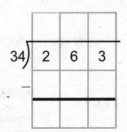

f) $\begin{array}{r} 9 \\ 44\overline{)362} \\ -396 \\ \hline \end{array}$
negative number!
TOO HIGH!

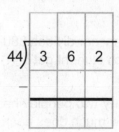

3. Divide.

a) 291 ÷ 43

b) 784 ÷ 85

c) 473 ÷ 67

d) 658 ÷ 74

4. Circle the first part of the dividend that is at least as big as the divisor.

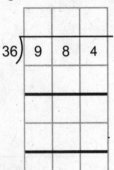

divisor

dividend

a) 48) ⓺③2 1

b) 73) 5 1 2 3

c) 27) 2 7 4 9

5. Estimate how many times 26 goes into the circled number. Multiply to check your estimate.

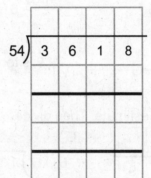

a)
```
      2
26 ) ⑥①3 2
   - 5 2
      9
```

b) 26) ⑭②7

c) 26) ⑧④7 6

6. Divide using long division. Hint: Circle the first part of the dividend that is at least as big as the divisor.

a)

36) 9 8 4

b)

54) 3 6 1 8

c)

36) 2 3 7 6

d) 17.28 ÷ 2.4

e) 168 ÷ 0.48

f) 15.37 ÷ 0.053

7. a) Is your answer to 2,376 ÷ 36 greater than your answer to 984 ÷ 36? _____

b) Explain why a student who answered "no" to part a) should look for a mistake.

8. a) Use long division to find 854 divided by 10. Write your answer ...

i) with a remainder.　　　ii) as a mixed number.　　　iii) as a decimal.

b) How could you have predicted the answer to part iii)?

9. A teacher divides 360 crackers among 24 students. How many crackers does each student get?

10. Thirty-two people share the total cost of a bus trip: $2,144.00. How much does each person pay?

11. Trisha has $14.45. How many $0.85 pencils can she buy?

12. How many books that are 0.25 inches thick will fit along a book shelf that is 18.5 inches long?

1. 98% of Antarctica is covered in ice. What fraction of Antarctica is *not* covered in ice?

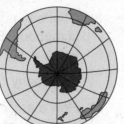

2. A ball is dropped from a height of 100 m.

Each time it hits the ground, it bounces $\frac{3}{5}$ of the height it fell from.

How high did it bounce …

a) on the first bounce?

b) on the second bounce?

3. The peel of a banana weighs $\frac{1}{8}$ of the total weight of the banana.

If you buy 4 kg of bananas at $0.60 per kg …

a) how much do you pay for the peel?

b) how much do you pay for the part you eat?

4. Janice earned $28.35 on Monday.

On Thursday, she spent $17.52 on a shirt.

She now has $32.23.

How much money did she have before she started work on Monday?

5. Jeff bought $\frac{8}{3}$ cups of berries. He used $\frac{1}{4}$ of the berries to bake a pie. He then ate $\frac{1}{6}$ of the pie. How many cups of berries did he eat?

6. Raya skated around a rink 8 times in $\frac{1}{3}$ of an hour. Each trip around the rink is 0.6 miles.

How far did Raya skate in an hour?

7. Six classes at George Washington P.S. are going skating.

There are 24 students in each class.
The teachers ordered 4 buses, which each hold 30 students. Will there be enough room? Explain.

8. It took Cindy 45 minutes to finish her homework. She spent $\frac{2}{5}$ of the time on math and $\frac{2}{5}$ of the time on history.

a) How many minutes did she spend on math and history?

b) How many minutes did she spend on other subjects?

c) What percent of the time did she spend on other subjects?

9. Anthony's taxi service charges $2.50 for the first kilometer and $1.50 for each additional kilometer. If Bob paid $17.50 in total, how many kilometers did he travel in the taxi?

10. Charlotte gave away 75% of her baseball cards.

a) What fraction of her cards did she keep?

b) Charlotte put her remaining cards in a scrapbook. Each page holds 14 cards and she filled 23 pages.

How many cards did she put in the book?

c) How many cards did she have before she gave part of her collection away?

11. Find the mystery numbers.

a) I am a number between 15 and 25.
I am a multiple of 3 and 4.

b) I am a number between 20 and 30.
My tens digit is 1 less than my ones digit.

c) Rounded to the nearest tens, I am 60.
I am an odd number.
The difference in my digits is 2.

12. A pentagonal box has a perimeter of 3.85 m. How long is each side?

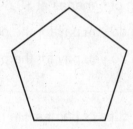

13. Will bought a binder for $17.25 and a pen for $2.35. He paid 15% in taxes.

How much change did he receive from $25.00?

14. Tom spent $500 on furniture: he spent $\frac{3}{10}$ of the money on a chair, $50.00 on a table, and the rest on a sofa.

What fraction and what percent of the $500.00 did he spend on each item?

15. a) Encke's Comet appears in our sky every 3.3 years.
How many times will it appear in a century?

b) A leap year happens every 4 years.
How many times will a leap year happen in a century?

c) Which answer is greater, a) or b)?
Why does this make sense?

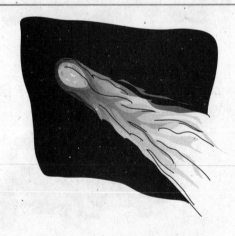

16. The heart pumps about 0.06 L of blood with each beat. About how many times would the heart need to beat to pump a liter of blood?

RP6-23 Ratios and Rates with Fractional Terms

> **REMINDER ▶•** $\dfrac{1}{5}$ of 5 = 1, so $\dfrac{3}{5}$ of 5 = 3 × 1 = 3

1. Find …

a) $\dfrac{4}{7}$ of 7 = *4 × 1 = 4*   b) $\dfrac{2}{6}$ of 6 =   c) $\dfrac{4}{5}$ of 5 =

d) $\dfrac{8}{3}$ of 3 =   e) $\dfrac{9}{8}$ of 8 =   **BONUS ▶** $\dfrac{13}{37}$ of 37 =

> **REMINDER ▶** $\dfrac{3}{5}$ × 5 = $\dfrac{3}{5}$ of 5 = 3 × 1 = 3

2. Find …

a) $\dfrac{5}{7}$ × 7 = _*5 × 1 = 5*_   b) $\dfrac{3}{4}$ × 4 = _____   c) $\dfrac{3}{8}$ × 8 = _____

d) $\dfrac{4}{5}$ × 5 = _____   e) $\dfrac{6}{5}$ × 5 = _____   **BONUS ▶** $\dfrac{18}{123}$ × 123 = _____

3. Find the number that makes the equation true and write it in the box.

a) ☐ × $\dfrac{1}{3}$ = 1   b) ☐ × $\dfrac{4}{5}$ = 4   c) ☐ × $\dfrac{3}{6}$ = 3

d) $\dfrac{5}{8}$ × ☐ = 5   e) ☐ × $\dfrac{3}{2}$ = 3   f) $\dfrac{7}{11}$ × ☐ = 7

> **REMINDER ▶** In a ratio table, you multiply each number in a row by the same number to get another row.

4. Find the missing number in the ratio table. Use the column that is full to find the number you should multiply by in the other column. Sometimes, the arrows may point from bottom to top.

a)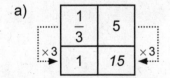

$\frac{1}{3}$	5
1	*15*
×3 →   ← ×3

b)

$\frac{1}{2}$	4
1	

c)

5	$\frac{2}{3}$
	2

d)

$\frac{4}{5}$	2
4	

e)

$\frac{3}{4}$	9
3	

f)

$\frac{1}{6}$	2
	12

g)

3	$\frac{2}{9}$
27	

h)

7	$\frac{2}{3}$
21	

i)

1	8
$\frac{1}{4}$	2
×4 →   ← ×4

j)

3	
$\frac{3}{4}$	9

k)

	6
$\frac{1}{2}$	3

l)

$\frac{3}{5}$	7
3	

6-23 Ratios and Rates with Fractional Terms

$1:6$ and $\frac{1}{2}:3$ are **equivalent ratios** because they show the same ratio.

For example, if there are 6 slices in a pizza, then half a pizza has 3 slices. $1:6$ $\frac{1}{2}:3$

5. Find the equivalent ratio using a ratio table. Sometimes, the arrows may point from bottom to top.

a)
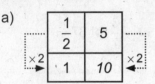

$\frac{1}{2}$	5
1	10

So, $\frac{1}{2}:5 = 1:\underline{\ 10\ }$

b)

$\frac{1}{3}$	4
1	

So, $\frac{1}{3}:4 = 1:\underline{\ \ \ }$

c)

6	$\frac{1}{4}$
	1

So, $6:\frac{1}{4} = \underline{\ \ \ }:1$

d)

$\frac{1}{7}$	4
1	

So, $\frac{1}{7}:4 = 1:\underline{\ \ \ }$

e)

1	
$\frac{1}{3}$	2

So, $1:\underline{\ \ \ } = \frac{1}{3}:2$

f)

1	
$\frac{1}{2}$	3

So, $1:\underline{\ \ \ } = \frac{1}{2}:3$

g)

10	1
	$\frac{1}{10}$

So, $10:1 = \underline{\ \ \ }:\frac{1}{10}$

h)

	$\frac{1}{3}$
12	1

So, $\underline{\ \ \ }:\frac{1}{3} = 12:1$

6. Make both terms a whole number without changing the ratio.

a) 5 mi run in $\frac{1}{2}$ hour

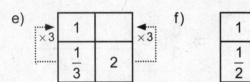

$$5 \ : \ \frac{1}{2}$$
$$\xrightarrow{\times 2}\ 10 \ : \ 1 \ \xleftarrow{\times 2}$$

b) 2 mi rowed in $\frac{1}{3}$ hour

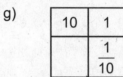

$$2 \ : \ \frac{1}{3}$$

$$\underline{\ \ \ } \ : \ \underline{\ \ \ }$$

c) $\frac{1}{4}$ cup of raisins for 2 cups of oats

$$\frac{1}{4} \ : \ 2$$

$$\underline{\ \ \ } \ : \ \underline{\ \ \ }$$

d) 4 mi per $\frac{1}{5}$ gal of gas

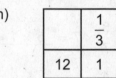

$$4 \ : \ \frac{1}{5}$$

$$\underline{\ \ \ } \ : \ \underline{\ \ \ }$$

7. Write an equivalent ratio with one term equal to 1.

a) $\frac{1}{3}:2 = \frac{1}{3} \times 3 : 2 \times 3 = \underline{\ 1\ }:\underline{\ 6\ }$

b) $3:\frac{1}{5} = 3 \times \underline{\ \ \ }:\frac{1}{5} \times \underline{\ \ } = \underline{\ \ \ }:\underline{\ \ \ }$

c) $\frac{1}{4}:3 =$

d) $5:\frac{1}{6} =$

e) $\frac{1}{11}:4 =$

BONUS ▶ $\frac{1}{2}:\frac{1}{3} =$

8. What would you multiply the rate by to make one term equal to 1?

	Rate	Rough Work	Answer
a)	2 km in $\frac{1}{3}$ h	$= 2$ km $\times$ ☐3☐ : $\frac{1}{3}$ h $\times$ ☐3☐	2 km : $\frac{1}{3}$ h = *6 km : 1 h*
b)	4 mi in $\frac{1}{2}$ h	$= 4$ mi $\times$ ☐ : $\frac{1}{2}$ h $\times$ ☐	4 mi : $\frac{1}{2}$ h =
c)	$\frac{1}{5}$ cups of oil for 4 eggs	$= \frac{1}{5}$ cups $\times$ ☐ : 4 eggs $\times$ ☐	$\frac{1}{5}$ cups : 4 eggs =
d)	$\frac{1}{4}$ h for 3 tasks	$= \frac{1}{4}$ h $\times$ ☐ : 3 tasks $\times$ ☐	$\frac{1}{4}$ h : 3 tasks =

A granola recipe uses $\frac{1}{2}$ cup of raisins for every 3 cups of oats. Ann wants to know how many cups of oats are needed for 1 cup of raisins. She finds an equivalent ratio using a ratio table:

Step 1: Ann makes a ratio table showing the cups of raisins for cups of oats.

Cups of Raisins	Cups of Oats
$\frac{1}{2}$	3
1	

Step 2: She finds the number being multiplied by in the first column. Then she multiplies by that number in the second column.

Therefore, $\frac{1}{2} : 3 = 1 : 6$ and she needs 6 cups of oats.

Cups of Raisins	Cups of Oats
$\frac{1}{2}$	3
1	6

×2 (left)   ×2 (right)

9. Solve by finding the equivalent ratio.

a) A plant grows $\frac{1}{2}$ cm in 4 days. How many days will it take to grow 1 cm?

cm	days
$\frac{1}{2}$	4
1	

b) Rhonda can ride her bike 3 km in $\frac{1}{4}$ of an hour. How far can she ride in 1 hour?

km	hours
3	$\frac{1}{4}$

c) On a map, $\frac{1}{5}$ cm represents 10 km. How many meters does 1 cm on the map represent?

d) A recipe uses $\frac{1}{3}$ cup milk and 2 cups flour. How much milk do you need if you use 6 cups of flour?

RP6-24 Unit Rates with Fractional and Decimal Terms

1. Divide to find the missing information. Write your answer as a mixed number.

   a) ┄┄ 4 mangoes cost $19

   ÷4 ⟶ 1 mango costs $\$\dfrac{19}{4}$ = $\$4\dfrac{3}{4}$

   b) 5 cakes cost $16

   1 cake costs ☐ = ☐

   c) 10 notebooks cost $24

   1 notebook costs ☐ = ☐

   d) 4 jackets cost $50

   1 jacket costs ☐ = ☐

2. Convert the fraction part to a decimal fraction in each part of Question 1, and then write the answer as a decimal number.

   a) $\$4\dfrac{3}{4} = \$4\dfrac{75}{100} = \$4.75$

   b)

   c)

   d)

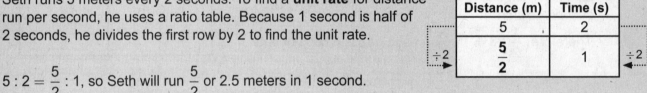

Seth runs 5 meters every 2 seconds. To find a **unit rate** for distance run per second, he uses a ratio table. Because 1 second is half of 2 seconds, he divides the first row by 2 to find the unit rate.

Distance (m)	Time (s)
5	2
$\dfrac{5}{2}$	1

$5 : 2 = \dfrac{5}{2} : 1$, so Seth will run $\dfrac{5}{2}$ or 2.5 meters in 1 second.

3. Find the unit rate using the ratio table.

   a)
3	5
1	$\dfrac{5}{3}$

   ÷3 ⟶   ⟵ ÷3

   $3 : 5 = 1 : \boxed{\dfrac{5}{3}}$

   b)
7	2
1	

   $7 : 2 = 1 : \boxed{}$

   c)
5	4
1	

   $5 : 4 = 1 : \boxed{}$

   d)
5	4
	1

   $5 : 4 = \boxed{} : 1$

   e)
1	
4	10

   ÷4 ⟶   ⟵ ÷4

   $1 : \boxed{} = 4 : 10$

   f)
1	
5	3

   $1 : \boxed{} = 5 : 3$

   g)
	1
7	5

   $\boxed{} : 1 = 7 : 5$

   BONUS ▶
1	
2	$\dfrac{2}{3}$

   $1 : \boxed{} = 2 : \dfrac{2}{3}$

4. Write the fraction that completes the unit rate.

a) 4 hours to walk 10 miles

$$4 : 10 = 1 : \boxed{\dfrac{10}{4}}$$

b) 3 wins for every 5 games played

$$3 : 5 = \boxed{} : 1$$

c) 2 cups of raisins for 7 cups of flour

$$2 : 7 = 1 : \boxed{}$$

d) 15 minutes to answer 4 questions

$$15 : 4 = \boxed{} : 1$$

5. Convert each fraction in Question 4 to a decimal fraction, and then write the answer as a decimal.

a) $\dfrac{10}{4} \xrightarrow[\times 25]{\times 25} \dfrac{250}{100} = 2.5$

$$4 : 10 = 1 : \boxed{2.5}$$

b) $\underline{} = \underline{} =$

$$3 : 5 = \boxed{} : 1$$

c) $\underline{} = \underline{} =$

$$2 : 7 = 1 : \boxed{}$$

d) $\underline{} = \underline{} =$

$$15 : 4 = \boxed{} : 1$$

6. Use a ratio table to find the unit rate in two steps.

a)

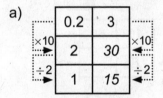

0.2	3
2	30
1	15

×10, ÷2

$0.2 : 3 = 1 : \underline{15}$

b)

0.5	3
5	
1	

$0.5 : 3 = 1 : \underline{}$

c)

2	0.4
	4
	1

$2 : 0.4 = \underline{} : 1$

d)

0.3	6
3	
1	

$0.3 : 6 = 1 : \underline{}$

e)

0.6	9
6	
1	

$0.6 : 9 = 1 : \underline{}$

f)

0.8	4
8	
1	

$0.8 : 4 = 1 : \underline{}$

g)

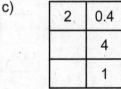

3	0.6
	6
	1

$3 : 0.6 = \underline{} : 1$

BONUS ▶

0.2	0.8
2	
1	

$0.2 : 0.8 = 1 : \underline{}$

RP6-25 Proportions and Word Problems

A **proportion** is an equation that shows two equivalent ratios. For example, 1 : 3 = 2 : 6 is a proportion.

To solve a proportion, you need to find the number you multiply (or divide) each term in one ratio by to get the other ratio. Proportions are easier to solve if you write the proportions using ratio tables.

For example, to solve 3 : 5 = 30 : ☐, Gabby uses a ratio table:

	3	5	
×10	30	**50**	×10

The missing number is 50, so 3 : 5 = 30 : 50.

1. Complete the ratio table. Write the numbers you multiply by on the arrows.
   Sometimes, the arrows may point from bottom to top.

   a)

   b)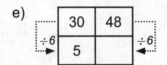

   c)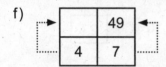

   d)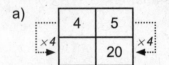

   e)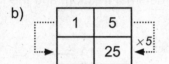

   f)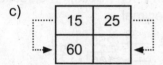

   g)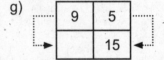

   h)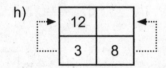

   BONUS ▶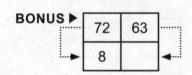

2. Use the ratio table to solve the proportion.

   a) 6 : 24 = ☐2☐ : 8
   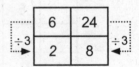

   b) ☐ : 20 = 2 : 5
   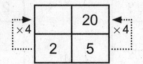

   c) 16 : 50 = 8 : ☐
   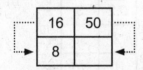

   d) 3 : 5 = ☐ : 30
   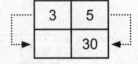

   e) ☐ : 33 = 3 : 11
   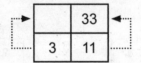

   f) 72 : 18 = ☐ : 3
   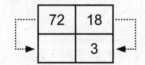

3. Decide which way the arrows point. Then solve the proportion.

   a)
10	
40	12

   b)
35	
7	10

   c)
18	22
9	

   d)
7	
42	24

   e)
15	21
5	

   f)
8	10
56	

4. Find the numbers that make the equation true and write them in the boxes.

a) $2 \times \dfrac{\boxed{7}}{\boxed{2}} = 7$

b) $3 \times \dfrac{\boxed{}}{\boxed{}} = 5$

c) $7 \times \dfrac{\boxed{}}{\boxed{}} = 11$

d) $3 \times \dfrac{\boxed{}}{\boxed{}} = 8$

e) $5 \times \dfrac{\boxed{}}{\boxed{}} = 9$

f) $12 \times \dfrac{\boxed{}}{\boxed{}} = 20$

5. Solve the following proportions. Sometimes you need to multiply by a fraction. Sometimes the arrows point from bottom to top.

a)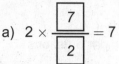

b)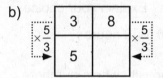

c)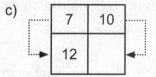

d)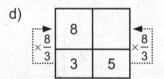

e)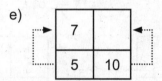

BONUS ▶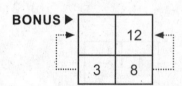

Jeff makes punch by mixing 2 cups of cranberry juice with 5 cups of ginger ale. How many cups of ginger ale does Jeff need to mix with 3 cups of cranberry juice?

Jeff makes a ratio table.
He finds the fraction being multiplied by in the first column.
Then he multiplies by that fraction in the second column.

$2 : 5 = 3 : \dfrac{15}{2}$, so Jeff needs $\dfrac{15}{2}$ (or $7\dfrac{1}{2}$) cups of ginger ale.

Cups of Cranberry Juice	Cups of Ginger Ale
2	5
3	$\dfrac{15}{2}$

$\times \dfrac{3}{2}$

---

6. Use Jeff's method to answer the question.

a) If 4 mangoes cost $6, how much do 6 mangoes cost?

Mangoes	Cost ($)
4	6
6	

b) Jackie can bike 6 km in 15 minutes. How long will it take Jackie to bike 10 km?

Distance (km)	Time (min)
6	15

c) Two out of every 6 people at a concert are seniors. There are 9 seniors at the concert. How many people are at the concert altogether?

d) Julie has 4 red marbles for every 6 blue marbles in her bag. She has 15 blue marbles. How many red marbles does she have?

RP6-26 Using Unit Rates to Solve Problems

1. Divide to find the missing information.

a) 4 tickets cost $68

1 ticket costs $ _____

b) 3 jackets cost $135

1 jacket costs $ _____

c) 144 miles per 6 gallons

_____ miles per 1 gallon

2. Find the unit rate.

a) 42 L of water in 3 jugs

_____ L of water in 1 jug

b) $112 for 7 hours

$ _____ for 1 hour

c) 456 miles in 8 hours

_____ miles in 1 hour

3. Which is the best deal for renting bicycles? Explain your choice.

A. $15 for 2 hours

B. $20 for 3 hours

C. $25 for 4 hours

4. Multiply by the same number to find a ratio with whole numbers.

a) $1 : \frac{1}{4}$

b) $2 : \frac{1}{3}$

c) $\frac{1}{2} : 5$

d) $2 : \frac{3}{4}$

5. Solve the proportion by using the ratio table.

a) $9 : 24 = \boxed{3} : 8$

b) $\boxed{} : 40 = 4 : 10$

c) $35 : \boxed{} = 5 : 7$

d) $7 : 3 = \boxed{} : 30$

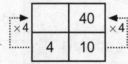

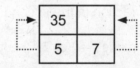

Sometimes you can solve a proportion by first reducing the ratio to lowest terms.

e) $8 : 10 = \boxed{12} : 15$

f) $\boxed{} : 30 = 40 : 50$

g) $11 : 22 = 5 : \boxed{}$

h) $6 : 24 = \boxed{} : 16$

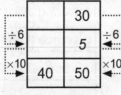

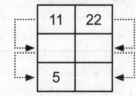

i) $15 : 20 = \boxed{} : 12$

j) $\boxed{} : 12 = 10 : 15$

k) $5 : 15 = \boxed{} : 21$

l) $6 : 9 = 10 : \boxed{}$

Allen makes orange paint by mixing 2 cups of red paint with 5 cups of yellow paint. How many cups of yellow paint does he need to mix with 3 cups of red paint?

Allen uses a ratio table to find a unit rate first and then the answer:

Step 1: He makes a ratio table.
He finds the number being divided by in the first column.
Then he divides by that number in the second column.

Red Paint	Yellow Paint
2	5
1	2.5

÷2   ÷2

Step 2: He adds another row to the ratio table and finds the number being multiplied by in the first column. Then he multiplies by that number in the second column.

Red Paint	Yellow Paint
2	5
1	2.5
3	**7.5**

×3   ×3

So, 2 : 5 = 3 : 7.5. Allen needs 7.5 cups of yellow paint.

---

6. John makes fruit salad. He needs 7 cups of apples for every 2 cups of strawberries.
   Complete the ratio table to find how many cups of apples he needs for 5 cups of strawberries.

Cups of Strawberries	Cups of Apples
2	7
1	
5	

So, 2 : 7 = 5 : _____ and John needs _____ cups of apples.

7. Use Allen's method to answer the question.

   a) Aisha runs 4 laps in 10 minutes.
      How long will it take her to run 6 laps?

Laps	Time (min)
4	10
1	
6	

   b) If 6 bus tickets cost $9, how much do 8 bus tickets costs?

Bus Tickets	Cost ($)
6	9

   c) Sophia has 4 jazz CDs for every 6 rock CDs. She has 15 rock CDs. How many jazz CDs does she have?

   d) Two out of every 6 students are boys. There are 9 boys in a class. How many students are in the class?

RP6-27 Changing US Customary Units of Length

3 feet is equal to 1 yard. Darya uses a ratio table to find how many yards are in 21 feet.

Step 1: She makes a ratio table for feet and yards.

Feet	Yards
3	1
21	

Step 2: She finds the number being multiplied by in the first column. Then she multiplies by that number in the second column.

So, 21 feet is equal to 7 yards.

×7 →

Feet	Yards
3	1
21	7

← ×7

1. Use Darya's method to change the measurements.

a) Change 15 feet to yards.

Feet	Yards
3	1
15	

15 ft = _____ yd

b) Change 9 yards to feet.

Feet	Yards
3	1
	9

_____ ft = 9 yd

c) Change 36 feet to yards.

Feet	Yards
3	1
36	

36 ft = _____ yd

REMINDER ▶ 1 mile = 1,760 yards, 1 yard = 3 feet, 1 foot = 12 inches

---

d) Change 2 miles to yards.

Miles	Yards
1	1,760

2 mi = _____ yd

e) Change 63 feet to yards.

Feet	Yards

63 ft = _____ yd

f) Change 72 inches to feet.

Inches	Feet

72 in = _____ ft

g) Change 12 feet to inches.

Feet	Inches

12 ft = _____ in

h) Change 5 miles to yards.

Miles	Yards

5 mi = _____ yd

i) Change 5,280 yards to miles.

Yards	Miles

5,280 yd = _____ mi

j) Change 99 feet to yards.

k) Change 75 feet to yards.

l) Change 17,600 yards to miles.

m) Change 45 yards to feet.

n) Change 144 inches to feet.

o) Change 30 feet to inches.

BONUS ▶

p) Change 18 inches to feet.

q) Change 5 feet to yards.

r) Change 4,400 yards to miles.

2. Divide to write each improper fraction as a mixed number.

a) $15 \div 2 = \underline{7}$ R $\underline{1}$ b) $53 \div 4 = \underline{}$ R $\underline{}$ c) $51 \div 8 = \underline{}$ R $\underline{}$ d) $33 \div 8 = \underline{}$ R $\underline{}$

So, $\dfrac{15}{2} = 7\dfrac{1}{2}$ So, $\dfrac{53}{4} =$ So, $\dfrac{51}{8} =$ So, $\dfrac{33}{8} =$

3. Multiply, and then write the answer as a mixed number.

a) $\dfrac{1}{2} \times 3 = \dfrac{3}{2}$ b) $\dfrac{5}{8} \times 3 = \underline{}$ c) $\dfrac{5}{8} \times 12 = \underline{}$ d) $\dfrac{3}{4} \times 12 = \underline{}$

$= 1\dfrac{1}{2}$ $=$ $=$ $=$

4. a) 1 mile = 1,760 yards

$\dfrac{1}{4}$ mi $= \dfrac{1}{4} \times 1{,}760$ yd $= \underline{}$ yd

b) 1 yard = 3 feet

$\dfrac{1}{2}$ yd $= \dfrac{1}{2} \times \underline{}$ ft $= \boxed{}$ ft

5. Convert from feet to inches.

a) $2\dfrac{3}{8}$ ft

2 ft $= \underline{2} \times \underline{12}$ in $= \underline{24}$ in

$\dfrac{3}{8}$ ft $= \boxed{\dfrac{3}{8}} \times \underline{12}$ in $= \boxed{4\dfrac{1}{2}}$ in

So, $2\dfrac{3}{8}$ ft $= \underline{24}$ in $+ \boxed{4\dfrac{1}{2}}$ in $= \boxed{28\dfrac{1}{2}}$ in

b) $2\dfrac{3}{4}$ ft

2 ft $= \underline{} \times \underline{}$ in $= \underline{}$ in

$\dfrac{3}{4}$ ft $= \boxed{} \times \underline{}$ in $= \underline{}$ in

So, $2\dfrac{3}{4}$ ft $= \underline{}$ in $+ \underline{}$ in $= \underline{}$ in

c) $5\dfrac{1}{2}$ ft

5 ft $= \underline{} \times \underline{}$ in $= \underline{}$ in

$\dfrac{1}{2}$ ft $= \boxed{} \times \underline{}$ in $= \underline{}$ in

So, $5\dfrac{1}{2}$ ft $= \underline{}$ in $+ \underline{}$ in $= \underline{}$ in

d) $4\dfrac{1}{4}$ ft

4 ft $= \underline{} \times \underline{}$ in $= \underline{}$ in

$\dfrac{1}{4}$ ft $= \boxed{} \times \underline{}$ in $= \underline{}$ in

So, $4\dfrac{1}{4}$ ft $= \underline{}$ in $+ \underline{}$ in $= \underline{}$ in

e) $6\dfrac{5}{8}$ ft

6 ft $= \underline{} \times \underline{}$ in $= \underline{}$ in

$\dfrac{5}{8}$ ft $= \boxed{} \times \underline{}$ in $= \boxed{}$ in

So, $6\dfrac{5}{8}$ ft $= \underline{}$ in $+ \boxed{}$ in $= \boxed{}$ in

f) $10\dfrac{7}{8}$ ft

10 ft $= \underline{} \times \underline{}$ in $= \underline{}$ in

$\dfrac{7}{8}$ ft $= \boxed{} \times \underline{}$ in $= \boxed{}$ in

So, $10\dfrac{7}{8}$ ft $= \underline{}$ in $+ \boxed{}$ in $= \boxed{}$ in

RP6-28 Using Unit Rates to Convert Measurements

Jane knows every 10 millimeters is 1 centimeter. To convert 25 millimeters to centimeters, she uses a ratio table:

Step 1: She makes a ratio table to find the unit rate.

$1 \div 10 = 0.1$, so each millimeter is 0.1 cm.

mm	cm
10	1
1	**0.1**

$\div 10$ $\div 10$

Step 2: She adds another row to the ratio table and converts 25 mm to centimeters.

$0.1 \times 25 = 2.5$, so 25 mm = 2.5 cm.

mm	cm
10	1
1	0.1
25	**2.5**

$\times 25$ $\times 25$

1. Use the unit rate to convert the measurements. Write your answer as a decimal.

a) 53 mm to cm

mm	cm
10	1
1	
53	

b) 6,900 g to kg

g	kg
1,000	1
1	

c) 3,200 m to km

m	km
1,000	1

d) 145 cm to m

cm	m

e) 454 g to kg

g	kg

f) 36 cm to m

cm	m

2. Answer the problem by changing the ratio into a unit rate. Write your answer as a decimal.

a) On a map, 3 cm represents 15 km. How many kilometers does 19.5 cm on the map represent?

cm on map	km
3	15
1	
19.5	

BONUS ▶ 5 cups hold 1,200 mL of water. How much water does 12.5 cups hold?

cups	mL
5	1,200
1	

Bob knows every 8 kilometers is 5 miles. To convert 20 km to miles, he uses a ratio table.

Step 1: He makes a ratio table to find the unit rate.

$5 \div 8 = \dfrac{5}{8}$, so each kilometer is $\dfrac{5}{8}$ mi.

km	mi
8	5
1	$\dfrac{5}{8}$

$\div 8$ $\div 8$

Step 2: He adds another row to the ratio table and converts 20 km to miles.

$\dfrac{5}{8} \times 20 = \dfrac{100}{8} = \dfrac{25}{2} = 12\dfrac{1}{2}$; therefore, 20 km is $12\dfrac{1}{2}$ mi.

km	mi
8	5
1	$\dfrac{5}{8}$
20	$12\dfrac{1}{2}$

$\times 20$ $\times 20$

3. Use the unit rate to convert the measurements. Write your answer as a mixed number.

a) 30 km to mi

km	mi
8	5
1	
30	

b) 4 mi to km

mi	km
5	8
1	
4	

c) 12 mi to km

mi	km
5	8
1	
12	

d) 25 km to mi

e) 13 mi to km

BONUS ▶ 100 km to mi

4. Convert the measurements. Remember: 1 yard = 3 feet. Write your answer as a mixed number.

a) 10 feet to yards

ft	yd
3	1
1	$\dfrac{1}{3}$
10	

b) $5\dfrac{1}{2}$ yards to feet

yd	ft
1	3
5	15

yd	ft
1	3
$\dfrac{1}{2}$	$\dfrac{3}{2} = 1\dfrac{1}{2}$

$15 + 1\dfrac{1}{2} = 16\dfrac{1}{2}$, so $5\dfrac{1}{2}$ yards is $16\dfrac{1}{2}$ feet

c) 23 feet to yards

d) $2\dfrac{3}{4}$ yards to feet

e) 100 feet to yards

5. Convert the measurements. Remember: 12 inches = 1 foot. Write your answer as a mixed number.

a) 18 inches to feet

in	ft
12	1
1	
18	

b) $2\dfrac{1}{4}$ feet to inches

ft	in
1	12
2	

ft	in
1	12
$\dfrac{1}{4}$	

c) 16 inches to feet

d) $3\dfrac{3}{4}$ feet to inches

e) 52 inches to feet

RP6-29 Tape Diagrams

Rita mixes 4 cups of mango juice with 3 cups of orange juice to make fruit punch. She uses a **tape diagram** to represent the mixture:

Mango juice: ▨▨▨▨   *The total amount of the fruit punch*
Orange juice: ▢▢▢   *has 7 **equal** parts.*

A tape diagram has two (or more) strips, one on top of the other. The strips are made of units of the same size.

1. Use a tape diagram to represent the number of boys and girls.

   a) The ratio of girls to boys is 3 : 2.

   girls: ▢▢▢   _3_ girls and

   boys: ▢▢   _2_ boys

   for every _5_ students

   b) The ratio of girls to boys is 2 : 3.

   girls: ___ girls and

   boys: ___ boys

   for every ___ students

   c) The ratio of boys to girls is 1 : 3.

   girls: ___ girls and

   boys: ___ boys

   for every ___ students

   d) The ratio of girls to boys is 3 : 4.

   girls: ___ girls and

   boys: ___ boys

   for every ___ students

   e) $\frac{3}{5}$ are girls.

   girls: ▢▢▢   ___ girls and

   boys: ▢▢   ___ boys

   for every ___ students

   f) $\frac{3}{7}$ are boys.

   girls: ___ girls and

   boys: ___ boys

   for every ___ students

2. Use a tape diagram to represent the number of each part. Sometimes, there are more than two parts in a whole.

   a) The ratio of kiwis to limes is 4 : 3.

   kiwis: ▢▢▢▢   ___ kiwis and

   limes: ▢▢▢   ___ limes

   for every ___ fruit

   b) $\frac{1}{5}$ of the audience is students.

   students:

   non-students:

   c) There are 3 adults and 2 seniors for each child in the store.

   children: ▢   ___ child, ___ adults

   adults: ▢▢▢   and ___ seniors

   seniors: ▢▢   for every ___ people

   d) For each cup of orange juice, there are 4 cups of cranberry juice and 2 cups of apple juice.

   orange:

   cranberry:

   apple:

Using the recipe 4 cups of mango juice for 3 cups of orange juice, Rita makes 35 cups of punch in total. Rita uses a tape diagram and ratio tables to find how many cups of each juice she needs.

Step 1: She uses a tape diagram to find the ratio of each part to the whole.

Mango juice: *ratio of mango juice to punch is **4** :7*

Orange juice: *ratio of orange juice to punch is **3** :7*

Step 2: She uses two ratio tables to find how many cups of each juice.

Cups of Mango	Cups in Total
4	7
20	35

×5 →   ← ×5

Cups of Orange	Cups in Total
3	7
15	35

×5 →   ← ×5

Rita needs to mix 20 cups of mango juice and 15 cups of orange juice to make her punch.

3. Use a tape diagram to find the ratio, and then solve the problem.

a) In a pet shop, there are 3 cats for every 5 dogs. If there are 40 pets in the shop, how many dogs are there?

dogs:

cats: *ratio of dogs to pets is 5 : 8*

Dogs	Pets

b) There are 2 red fish for every 5 blue fish in an aquarium. If there are 21 fish in the aquarium, how many blue fish are in the aquarium?

Blue Fish	Total Fish

c) There are 35 children in a class. The ratio of girls to boys is 3 : 2. Determine the number of girls and boys in the class.

BONUS ▶ A punch recipe calls for 6 cups of mango juice and 2 cups of orange juice. How many cups of each juice do you need to make 20 cups of punch?

These are equivalent statements:

$\dfrac{6}{9}$ of the circles are shaded.

$\dfrac{2}{3}$ of the circles are shaded.

6 is $\dfrac{2}{3}$ of 9.

$6 : 9 = 2 : 3$

part   whole

1. Write four equivalent statements for the picture.

a)

$\dfrac{4}{6}$ _are shaded_

_____

$\dfrac{2}{3}$ _are shaded_

_____

4 is $\dfrac{2}{3}$ of 6

_____

$4 : 6 = 2 : 3$

_____

b)

_____

_____

_____

_____

c)

_____

_____

_____

_____

d)

_____

_____

_____

_____

2. For the picture, write a pair of equivalent ratios.

a)

4 is $\dfrac{1}{2}$ of 8

$\dfrac{4}{\text{part}} : \dfrac{8}{\text{whole}} = \dfrac{1}{} : \dfrac{2}{}$

b)

6 is $\dfrac{3}{5}$ of 10

$\dfrac{}{\text{part}} : \dfrac{}{\text{whole}} = \underline{} : \underline{}$

c)

2 is $\dfrac{1}{4}$ of 8

$\dfrac{}{\text{part}} : \dfrac{}{\text{whole}} = \underline{} : \underline{}$

3. For the statement, write a pair of equivalent ratios and equivalent fractions.

a) 15 is $\dfrac{3}{4}$ of 20 $\dfrac{}{\text{part}} : \dfrac{}{\text{whole}} = \underline{} : \underline{}$ $\dfrac{\text{part}}{\text{whole}}\ \underline{} = \underline{}$

b) 18 is $\dfrac{9}{10}$ of 20 $\dfrac{}{\text{part}} : \dfrac{}{\text{whole}} = \underline{} : \underline{}$ $\dfrac{\text{part}}{\text{whole}}\ \underline{} = \underline{}$

4. Fill in the blanks. Write a question mark where you are missing a piece of information.

a) 12 is $\frac{4}{5}$ of what number? $\dfrac{12}{\text{part}} : \dfrac{?}{\text{whole}} = \dfrac{4}{} : \dfrac{5}{}$ $\dfrac{\text{part}}{\text{whole}}$ $\dfrac{12}{?} = \dfrac{4}{5}$

b) 6 is how many quarters of 8? $\dfrac{6}{\text{part}} : \dfrac{8}{\text{whole}} = \dfrac{?}{} : \dfrac{4}{}$ $\dfrac{\text{part}}{\text{whole}}$ $\dfrac{}{} = \dfrac{}{}$

c) What is $\frac{3}{4}$ of 16? $\dfrac{}{\text{part}} : \dfrac{}{\text{whole}} = \dfrac{}{} : \dfrac{}{}$ $\dfrac{\text{part}}{\text{whole}}$ $\dfrac{}{} = \dfrac{}{}$

d) 20 is how many thirds of 30? $\dfrac{}{\text{part}} : \dfrac{}{\text{whole}} = \dfrac{}{} : \dfrac{}{}$ $\dfrac{\text{part}}{\text{whole}}$ $\dfrac{}{} = \dfrac{}{}$

5. For the statement, write a pair of equivalent ratios and a pair of equivalent fractions.

a) 15 is what percent of 20? $\dfrac{15}{\text{part}} : \dfrac{20}{\text{whole}} = \dfrac{?}{} : \dfrac{100}{}$ $\dfrac{\text{part}}{\text{whole}}$ $\dfrac{15}{20} = \dfrac{?}{100}$

b) What is 25% of 80? $\dfrac{}{\text{part}} : \dfrac{}{\text{whole}} = \dfrac{}{} : \dfrac{}{}$ $\dfrac{\text{part}}{\text{whole}}$ $\dfrac{}{} = \dfrac{}{}$

c) 18 is 3% of what number? $\dfrac{}{\text{part}} : \dfrac{}{\text{whole}} = \dfrac{}{} : \dfrac{}{}$ $\dfrac{\text{part}}{\text{whole}}$ $\dfrac{}{} = \dfrac{}{}$

6. Write the two pieces of information you are given and what you need to find (?). Then write an equation for the problem.

a) What percent of 25 is 5?   part __5__   whole __25__   percent __?__ $\dfrac{5}{25} = \dfrac{?}{100}$

b) If 7 is 20%, what is 100%?   part ____   whole __?__   percent ____ $\dfrac{}{?} = \dfrac{}{100}$

c) What is 18% of 25?   part __?__   whole ____   percent ____ $\dfrac{?}{} = \dfrac{}{100}$

d) If 3 is 12%, what is 100%?   part ____   whole ____   percent ____ $\dfrac{}{} = \dfrac{}{100}$

e) What percent of 50 is 4?   part ____   whole ____   percent ____ $\dfrac{}{} = \dfrac{}{100}$

Solve the proportion.

$\dfrac{3}{5} = \dfrac{?}{100}$

Step 1

Notice: $5 \times 20 = 100$

Step 2

Write what you would multiply by.

$\dfrac{3}{5} \begin{array}{c} \xrightarrow{\times 20} \\ = \\ \xrightarrow{\times 20} \end{array} \dfrac{?}{100}$

Step 3

$\dfrac{3}{5} = \dfrac{60}{100}$

---

7. Solve the proportions in Question 6 using the method above.

RP6-31 Cumulative Review

1. a) Use skip counting or multiplication to complete the ratio table.

7 : 2

7	2

b) Find the missing numbers in the ratio table.

3 : 5

3	5
6	
9	15
	20

2. a) Complete the table for the rate.

4 gifts for each student

# of Students	# of Gifts
1	4

b) Multiply to find the missing information.

180 km in 2 hours

_____ km in 6 hours

3. Find the missing numbers in the double number line diagram.

a)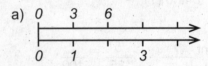

c)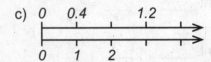

b)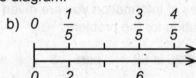

d)

4. Emma drives 50 miles every hour. She is driving to her parent's house 175 miles away. Use a double number line diagram to find out how long it will take her to get there.

5. Change the fraction to a percent by first reducing it to lowest terms.

a) $\frac{12}{16} = \frac{}{4} = \frac{}{100} = $ _____ %

b) $\frac{6}{30} = $

c) $\frac{14}{35} = $

d) $\frac{13}{26} = $

6. Change each number to a fraction. Then write the numbers in order from least to greatest.

45%, $\frac{3}{7}$, 0.4

Ratios and Proportional Relationships 6-31

7. a) To select new board members, the Sports Club held an election. 54 out of the 72 members of the Sports Club voted in the election. What percentage of the members voted?

b) 13 of the 52 audience members at the City Theatre are seniors. What percentage of the audience at the City Theatre is not seniors?

c) Juliet ordered chocolate chip cookies and oatmeal cookies for her class. She ordered 76 cookies in all. 38 of the cookies were oatmeal. What percentage of the cookies were chocolate chip?

d) 32 out of 32 students signed up for the field trip. What percentage of students signed up for the field trip?

8. Fill in the missing numbers for each classroom.

	Percent That Are Girls	Percent That Are Boys	Fraction That Are Girls	Fraction That Are Boys	Ratio of Girls to Boys
a)	40%		$\frac{40}{100}$		
b)				$\frac{45}{100}$	
BONUS ▶					12 : 13

9. Use a ratio table to find the unit rate, and then answer the question.

a) Sandy got $41.25 for 5 hours of work. How many hours does she need to work to earn $66?

Time (h)	Money ($)
5	41.25
1	
	66

b) If 9 pizza slices cost $15, how much does 12 pizza slices cost?

Pizza Slices	Cost ($)
9	15

c) Silvio has 2 science books for every 6 fiction books. He has 7 science books. How many fiction books does he have?

d) Six out of every 10 students are girls. There are 10 boys in a class. How many students are in the class?

10. Jack drives to his uncle's house 400 km away. He can drive half of the route at 100 km per hour and the other half at 80 km per hour. How long does it take him to get there?

11. Answer the problem by changing the ratio into a unit rate. Write your answer as a decimal.

a) On a map, 5 cm represent 15 km. How many kilometers does 22.5 cm on the map represent?

cm on map	km
5	15
1	
22.5	

BONUS ▶ 4 cups hold 1,400 mL of water. How much water does 12.5 cups hold?

cups	mL
4	1,400
1	

12. Convert the measurement. Remember: 1 yard = 3 feet. Write your answer as a mixed number.

a) 20 feet to yards

ft	yd
3	1
1	$\frac{1}{3}$
20	

b) $7\frac{1}{2}$ yards to feet

yd	ft
1	3
7	21

yd	ft
1	3
$\frac{1}{2}$	$\frac{3}{2} = 1\frac{1}{2}$

$21 + 1\frac{1}{2} = 22\frac{1}{2}$, so $7\frac{1}{2}$ yards is $22\frac{1}{2}$ feet

c) 32 feet to yards

d) $3\frac{1}{4}$ yards to feet

13. Convert the measurement. Remember: 12 inches = 1 foot. Write your answer as a mixed number.

a) 30 inches to feet

in	ft
12	1
1	
30	

b) $2\frac{3}{4}$ feet to inches

ft	in
1	12
2	

ft	in
1	12
$\frac{3}{4}$	

c) 16 inches to feet

d) $5\frac{1}{4}$ feet to inches

BONUS ▶ When 5 new students join a class that already has 15 boys and 12 girls, the number of boys increases by 20%. What is the new ratio of boys to girls?

EE6-8 Solving Equations—Preserving Equality

1. Write the number that makes the equation true.

a) $8 + 4 - \boxed{} = 8$ b) $8 \times 3 \div \boxed{} = 8$ c) $8 \div 2 \times \boxed{} = 8$

d) $12 \div 4 \times \boxed{} = 12$ e) $13 - 6 + \boxed{} = 13$ f) $19 + 3 - \boxed{} = 19$

2. Write the operation that makes the equation true.

a) $7 + 2 \bigcirc 2 = 7$ b) $8 \times 3 \bigcirc 3 = 8$ c) $12 \div 2 \bigcirc 2 = 12$

d) $15 - 4 \bigcirc 4 = 15$ e) $18 \div 3 \bigcirc 3 = 18$ f) $6 + 4 \bigcirc 4 = 6$

3. Write the operation and number that make the equation true.

a) $17 + 3 \underline{\ -3\ } = 17$ b) $20 \div 4 \underline{} = 20$ c) $18 \times 2 \underline{} = 18$

d) $11 - 4 \underline{} = 11$ e) $4 \times 3 \underline{} = 4$ f) $15 + 2 \underline{} = 15$

g) $5 \times 2 \underline{} = 5$ h) $5 \div 2 \underline{} = 5$ i) $5 - 2 \underline{} = 5$

j) $n + 3 \underline{\ -3\ } = n$ k) $n \times 3 \underline{} = n$ l) $5m \underline{} = m$

m) $x - 5 \underline{} = x$ n) $x + 7 \underline{} = x$ o) $z \div 5 \underline{} = z$

REMINDER ▶ The variable x represents a number, so you can treat it like a number.

Operation	Result	Operation	Result
Add 3 to x.	$x + 3$	Multiply 3 by x.	$3 \times x = 3x$
Add x to 3.	$3 + x$	Multiply x by 3.	$x \times 3 = 3x$
Subtract 3 from x.	$x - 3$	Divide x by 3.	$x \div 3$
Subtract x from 3.	$3 - x$	Divide 3 by x.	$3 \div x$

---

4. Show the result of the operation.

a) Multiply x by 7. $\underline{\quad 7x \quad}$ b) Add 4 to x. $\underline{\quad x + 4 \quad}$ c) Subtract 5 from x. $\underline{}$

d) Subtract x from 5. $\underline{}$ e) Divide x by 10. $\underline{}$ f) Divide 9 by x. $\underline{}$

g) Multiply 8 by x. $\underline{}$ h) Add x to 9. $\underline{}$ **BONUS** ▶ Add x to y. $\underline{}$

5. How could you undo the operation and get back to the number you started with?

a) add 4 $\underline{\ subtract\ 4\ }$ b) multiply by 3 $\underline{}$ c) subtract 9 $\underline{}$

d) divide by 2 $\underline{}$ e) add 7 $\underline{}$ f) multiply by 5 $\underline{}$

g) multiply by 2 $\underline{}$ h) divide by 8 $\underline{}$ i) subtract x $\underline{}$

6. Solve for x by doing the same thing to both sides of the equation. Check your answer.

a) $3x = 12$

$3x \div 3 = 12 \div 3$

$x = 4$

Check by replacing
x with your answer: $3\,(4) = 12$ ✓

b) $x \div 6 = 3$

$x \div 6 \times 6 = 3 \times 6$

c) $x - 4 = 20$

d) $x \div 3 = 5$

e) $12 + x = 22$

f) $44 = 4x$

g) $x - 17 = 25$

h) $31 = 19 + x$

i) $x + 26 = 53$

j) $11 = x \div 5$

k) $9x = 63$

BONUS ▶ $x + 9 = 9 + 45$

Eva solves $7 - x = 5$ in two steps.

Step 1: She treats x as a number and adds x to both sides:

$7 - x + x = 5 + x$

$7 = 5 + x$

Step 2: She subtracts 5 from both sides to find x:

$7 - 5 = 5 + x - 5$

$2 = x$

Eva checks her answer. She replaces x in the equation with 2: $7 - 2 = 5$ ✓

---

7. Solve the equation in two steps like Eva. Check your answer.

a) $12 - x = 6$

$12 - x + x = 6 + x$

$12 = 6 + x$

$12 - 6 = 6 + x - 6$

$6 = x$

Check by replacing
x with your answer: $12 - 6 = 6$ ✓

b) $6 = 13 - x$

c) $24 - x = 20$

d) $3 = 15 - x$

e) $59 - x = 56$

f) $26 = 43 - x$

g) $31 - x = 11$

h) $73 - x = 41$

i) $17 - x = 17$

EE6-9　Solving Equations—Using Logic

To solve the equation $x + 3 = 8$, Mike and Jill use different methods.

Mike uses preserving equality:

$$x + 3 = 8$$
$$x + 3 - 3 = 8 - 3$$
$$x = 5$$

Jill uses logic. She thinks about how addition and subtraction are related:

$x + 3 = 8$ means I have to add 3 to x to get 8.

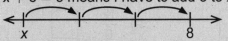

So, I have to subtract 3 from 8 to find x.

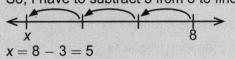

$$x = 8 - 3 = 5$$

1. Use Jill's method to solve the equation.

a) $x + 5 = 12$

$\quad x = 12 - 5$

$\quad x = 7$

b) $x + 3 = 10$

c) $x + 25 = 41$

d) $21 + x = 34$

e) $28 = 8 + x$

f) $41 = x + 14$

g) $17 + x = 56$

h) $x + 22 = 33$

i) $16 + x = 34$

j) $x + 35 = 61$

k) $6 + x = 100$

l) $5 + x + 2 = 18$

Mike and Jill solve the equation $x - 2 = 5$.

Mike uses preserving equality:

$$x - 2 = 5$$
$$x - 2 + 2 = 5 + 2$$
$$x = 7$$

Jill uses logic:

$x - 2 = 5$ means I have to subtract 2 from x to get 5.
So, I have to add 2 to 5 to find x.

$$x = 5 + 2 = 7$$

---

2. Use Jill's method to solve the equation.

a) $x - 5 = 12$

$\quad x = 12 + 5$

$\quad x = 17$

b) $x - 12 = 5$

c) $26 = x - 3$

d) $x - 19 = 9$

e) $x - 7 = 28$

f) $x - 13 = 22$

g) $14 = x - 27$

h) $29 = x - 32$

i) $x - 15 = 62$

j) $43 = x - 19$

k) $x - 51 = 49$

l) $73 = x - 21$

REMINDER ▶ Division is often written in fractional form.

Examples: $12 \div 4 = \dfrac{12}{4}$ $\quad$ $15 \div 5 = \dfrac{15}{5}$ $\quad$ $x \div 3 = \dfrac{x}{3}$ $\quad$ $w \div 7 = \dfrac{w}{7}$

3. Solve the division problem.

a) $\dfrac{6}{3} = \boxed{2}$ $\qquad$ b) $\dfrac{12}{6} = \boxed{}$ $\qquad$ c) $\dfrac{12}{4} = \boxed{}$ $\qquad$ d) $\dfrac{15}{5} = \boxed{}$

Mike and Jill solve the equation $3x = 12$.

Mike uses preserving equality: $\qquad\qquad$ Jill uses logic:

$\qquad\qquad 3x = 12$ $\qquad\qquad\qquad\qquad$ $3x = 12$ means I have to multiply x by 3 to get 12.
$\qquad 3x \div 3 = 12 \div 3$ $\qquad\qquad\qquad$ So, I have to divide 12 by 3 to find x.
$\qquad\qquad\quad x = 4$

$\qquad\qquad\qquad\qquad\qquad\qquad\qquad\qquad$ $x = 12 \div 3 = 4$

4. Use Mike's method to solve the equation by preserving equality.

a) $\quad 4x = 12$ $\qquad$ b) $2x = 10$ $\qquad$ c) $6x = 42$ $\qquad$ d) $2x = 14$

$\quad 4x \div 4 = 12 \div 4$

$\qquad\qquad x = 3$

e) $7x = 28$ $\qquad$ f) $6x = 18$ $\qquad$ g) $7x = 49$ $\qquad$ h) $8x = 48$

Mike and Jill solve the equation $\dfrac{x}{3} = 8$.

Mike uses preserving equality: $\qquad\qquad$ Jill uses logic:

$\qquad\qquad \dfrac{x}{3} = 8$ $\qquad\qquad\qquad\qquad\qquad$ $\dfrac{x}{3} = 8$ means I have to divide x by 3 to get 8.

$\qquad \dfrac{x}{3} \times 3 = 8 \times 3$ $\qquad\qquad\qquad$ So, I have to multiply 8 by 3 to find x.

$\qquad\qquad\quad x = 24$ $\qquad\qquad\qquad\qquad$ $x = 8 \times 3$, so $x = 24$

5. Solve the equation using logic.

a) $\dfrac{x}{2} = 3$ $\qquad$ b) $2x = 8$ $\qquad$ c) $\dfrac{x}{4} = 5$ $\qquad$ d) $3 + x = 8$ $\qquad$ e) $x - 5 = 6$

$x = 3 \times 2$

$x = 6$

f) $\dfrac{x}{3} = 4$ $\qquad$ g) $5 + x = 12$ $\qquad$ h) $12 = 2x$ $\qquad$ i) $15 = 3x$ $\qquad$ j) $4 = \dfrac{x}{5}$

k) $\dfrac{x}{7} = 4$ $\qquad$ l) $\dfrac{x}{4} = 7$ $\qquad$ m) $3x = 27$ $\qquad$ n) $36 = 12x$ $\qquad$ **BONUS** ▶ $\dfrac{x}{15} = 6$

EE6-10 Totals, Differences, and Equations

1. Fill in the table. Write *x* for the number you are not given.

		Blue Balloons	Red Balloons	Total Balloons	Another Way to Write the Total
a)	9 blue balloons 17 balloons in total	9	x	17	9 + x
b)	15 blue balloons 13 red balloons				
c)	31 balloons in total 18 blue balloons				
d)	17 red balloons 23 balloons altogether				
e)	34 red balloons 21 blue balloons				

When you can write the same number two ways, you can write an equation.

Example: 9 blue balloons, *x* red balloons, 17 balloons in total

Write the total two ways to get an equation: $9 + x = 17$

2. Circle the total in the story. Then write an equation.

a) ~~15 blue balloons~~
⟨**28 balloons altogether**⟩
x red balloons

$\underline{\quad 15 + x = 28 \quad}$

b) 12 blue balloons
14 red balloons
x balloons altogether

$\underline{\hspace{3cm}}$

c) 27 balloons altogether
19 red balloons
x blue balloons

$\underline{\hspace{3cm}}$

d) There are 13 red apples.
There are *x* green apples.
There are 27 apples in total.

$\underline{\hspace{3cm}}$

e) There are *x* red apples.
There are 14 green apples.
There are 39 apples in total.

$\underline{\hspace{3cm}}$

f) There are 55 red apples.
There are 16 green apples.
There are *x* apples in total.

$\underline{\hspace{3cm}}$

3. Circle the total in the story. Then write an equation and solve it.

a) There are 9 girls.
There are 12 boys.
There are *x* students altogether.

$\underline{\hspace{3cm}}$

b) There are 19 stickers.
x of them are black.
11 of them are not black.

$\underline{\hspace{3cm}}$

c) Jeff has 9 friends.
x of them are girls.
6 friends are boys.

$\underline{\hspace{3cm}}$

larger part − smaller part = difference

$$9 - x = 4$$

9 is 4 more than x. x is 4 fewer than 9.

---

4. Fill in the table. Write x for the number you are not given. Circle the larger part, and then write the difference another way.

		Parts		Difference	Another Way to Write the Difference
		Apples	Oranges		
a)	13 apples; 5 more oranges than apples	13	(x)	5	x − 13
b)	9 more oranges than apples; 12 apples				
c)	6 apples; 7 oranges				
d)	19 oranges; 8 fewer apples than oranges				
e)	27 oranges; 13 fewer oranges than apples				

5. Circle the part that is larger. Write the difference two ways to make an equation.

a) (8 apples)
3 fewer oranges than apples
x oranges

$$\underline{8 - x = 3}$$

b) 5 apples
13 oranges
x more oranges than apples

_____

c) 12 more apples than oranges
5 oranges
x apples

_____

6. Circle the part that is larger. Write the difference two ways to make an equation. Then solve the equation.

a) There are (7 CDs).
There are x books.
There are 5 more CDs than books.

b) There are x CDs.
There are 12 books.
There are 6 fewer CDs than books.

c) There are 12 CDs.
There are 29 books.
There are x fewer CDs than books.

d) There are 17 pens.
There are x pencils.
There are 8 more pens than pencils.

e) Tom has 19 stickers.
Amit has x stickers.
Tom has 13 fewer stickers than Amit.

f) Sophie's class has x students.
Amy's class has 34 students.
Sophie's class has 6 fewer students than Amy's class.

7. Fill in the table. Write x for the number you are not given.

	Problem	Parts	How Many?	Equation and Solution
a)	Alan has 22 jazz CDs in his collection. He has 8 more jazz CDs than pop CDs. How many pop CDs does he have?	jazz CDs	⃝22	$22 - x = 8$ $22 \quad = 8 + x$
		pop CDs	x	$22 - 8 = x$ $14 = x$
b)	Darya has 21 red balloons. She has 9 green balloons. How many more red balloons than green balloons does she have?			
c)	There are 7 apples in the fridge. There are 4 more oranges than apples in the fridge. How many oranges are there?			
d)	Female European wolves weigh 9 pounds less than male wolves. Males weigh 84 pounds. How much do females weigh?			

8. Write the difference two ways to write an equation. Then solve the equation.

a) Simone exercised for 25 minutes on Saturday. On Sunday she exercised for 17 minutes more than on Saturday. For how long did she exercise on Sunday?

$\underline{\quad x - 25 = 17 \quad}$

$\underline{\quad x = 17 + 25 \quad}$

$\underline{\quad = 42 \quad}$

b) There are 32 teachers in the school. There are 18 fewer volunteers than teachers. How many volunteers are there?

$\underline{\qquad\qquad\qquad}$

$\underline{\qquad\qquad\qquad}$

$\underline{\qquad\qquad\qquad}$

c) North American wolves weigh 79 pounds. Indian–Arabian wolves weigh 23 pounds less. How much do Indian–Arabian wolves weigh?

d) Jamal biked 13 km on Saturday. He biked 5 km more on Sunday than on Saturday. How many kilometers did he bike on Sunday?

e) Scott counted 68 cars in a parking lot on Monday and 39 cars on Tuesday. How many fewer cars were parked there on Tuesday?

f) Gabby's art exhibition had 658 visitors on the first night. The next night, there were 18 more visitors than on the first night. How many visitors came on the second night?

EE6-11 Addition and Subtraction Word Problems

1. Fill in the table. Write *x* for the number you need to find. Cross out the cell you do not use.

	Problem	Parts	How Many?	Difference / Total	Equation and Solution
a)	Greg has 2 dogs and 5 fish. How many pets does he have?	dogs	2	Difference: ~~___~~	$2 + 5 = x$
		fish	5	Total: _x_	$x = 7$
b)	Elise hiked 13 km on Saturday. She hiked 14 km on Sunday. How far did Elise hike in two days?			Difference: _____	
				Total: _____	
c)	Leila saved $43 in January. She saved $14 less in February than in January. How much money did she save in February?			Difference: _____	
				Total: _____	
d)	The Steel Dragon roller coaster in Japan is 318 ft tall. It is 138 ft shorter than the Kingda Ka in Jackson, NJ. How tall is the Kingda Ka roller coaster?			Difference: _____	
				Total: _____	
e)	A supermarket sold 473 bags of white and yellow potatoes. If 139 of the bags were filled with white potatoes, how many bags of yellow potatoes were sold?			Difference: _____	
				Total: _____	

2. Write the parts and how many of each part. Then write and solve an equation.

a) Clarence watched TV for 45 minutes. He spent 15 minutes less on his homework than on watching TV. How much time did he spend on homework?

b) A recreation pass costs $24. It is $9 more than a movie pass. How much do the two passes cost together?

c) The Mercury City Tower in Moscow is 339 m tall. The Willis Tower in Chicago is 442 m tall. How much taller is the Willis Tower than the Mercury City Tower?

Mercury City Tower   Willis Tower

3. Solve the problem using an equation for each part. Use your answer from part i) as data for part ii).

a) Alex read for 30 minutes before dinner and 45 minutes after dinner.

   i) How many minutes did he spend reading altogether?

   ii) Alex's dinner took 30 minutes. If he finished his after-dinner reading at 7:30 p.m., when did Alex start eating dinner?

b) There are 18 players on a soccer team. Seven of them are reserve players and the rest are field players.

   i) How many field players are on the team?

   ii) How many more field players than reserve players are on the team?

4. Solve the two-step problems.

a) Mariko bought 16 red stickers and 25 blue stickers. She used 13 of them. How many stickers does she have left?

b) There are 28 students in a sixth grade class. Thirteen of them are boys. How many more girls than boys are in the class?

c) Shawn read 7 mysteries. He read 3 more science fiction books than mysteries. How many books did he read altogether?

d) Anya had $75. She spent $12 on two shirts, $32 on shoes, and $25 on a jacket. How much money does she have left?

5. There are 23,500 houses and 12,700 apartments in a town.

a) How many houses and apartments are there in total?

b) How many more houses are there than apartments?

c) A company plans to tear down 750 houses and replace them with 2,400 apartments. How many more houses than apartments will there be?

6. The table shows Sam's savings account balances from June to August. She did not withdraw money from her savings account.

End of June	$237.57
End of July	$352.24
End of August	$528.06

a) How much did she deposit in July?

b) How much did she deposit in July and August altogether?

c) How much more did Sam deposit in August than in July?

EE6-12 Models and "Times as Many"

1. Draw a tape diagram to model the story.

   a) Sally has 7 stickers. Julie has 3 times as many stickers as Sally does.

      | Sally's stickers | | 7 | |
      | Julie's stickers | | 7 | 7 | 7 |

   b) There are 5 blue marbles. There are 4 times as many red marbles.

      _____

      _____

   c) There are 12 red apples. There are 4 times as many green apples as red apples.

      _____

      _____

   d) Pam has 4 stickers. Nancy has 5 times as many stickers.

      _____

      _____

2. Solve the problem by drawing a model.

   a) Jin has 5 stickers. Rob has 3 times as many stickers as Jin. How many stickers do they have together?

      | Jin's stickers: 5 | | 5 | |
      | Rob's stickers: 15 | | 5 | 5 | 5 |

      5 + 15 = 20, so Jin and Rob have

      20 stickers altogether.

   b) Rashid studies rats and hamsters. He has 7 rats and twice as many hamsters. How many animals does he have altogether?

      _____

      _____

      _____

   c) There are 12 chocolate chip cookies in a box. There are 6 times as many oatmeal cookies in the box. How many cookies are there altogether?

   d) There are 17 math books in a school library. There are 4 times as many science books in the library. How many math books and science books are in the library altogether?

3. Draw a model for the story. Then write the given number beside the correct bar.

   a) There are 24 mangoes. There are 4 times as many mangoes as avocados.

      | Mangoes: 24 | | | | | |
      | Avocados: | | | |

   b) There are 30 seniors in the audience. There are 6 times as many seniors as children.

      _____

      _____

   c) Majid spent $24.50 on shoes and twice as much on pants.

      _____

      _____

   d) Mina studied math for 30 minutes and science for 3 times as many minutes.

      _____

      _____

4. All blocks are the same size. What is the size of each block?

a)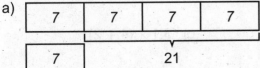

b)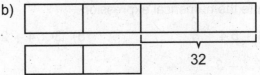

c)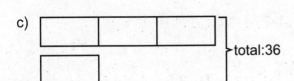

d)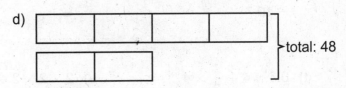

5. Draw the model. Find the length of one block in the model. Then solve the problem.

a) Jay has 3 times as many cards as Said. Jay has 12 more cards than Said. How many cards does each boy have?

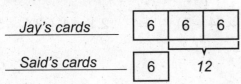

Jay has __18__ cards,

and Said has __6__ cards.

b) Peter is 4 times as old as Ella. Peter is 15 years older than Ella. How old are Peter and Ella?

_____

_____

Peter is ____ years old,

and Ella is ____ years old.

c) There are 6 times as many party balloons as streamers to decorate the house. There are 42 decorations altogether. How many balloons and how many streamers are there?

d) A pancake recipe calls for 2 tablespoons of butter and 3 times as many tablespoons of sugar. Anna wants to make 24 pancakes. How many tablespoons of sugar and butter does she need?

There are ____ party balloons

and ____ streamers.

Anna needs ____ tablespoons of butter and

____ tablespoons of sugar.

6. A pair of shoes costs twice as much as a wallet. George paid $52.50 for a pair of shoes and a wallet. How much does each item cost?

_____

_____

✎ **BONUS ▶** How much would George pay for two pairs of shoes and three wallets?

EE6-13 Evaluating Expressions

1. Calculate the numerical expression.

   a) $2.3 + 5.4 + 3$

   $= 7.7 + 3$

   $= 10.7$

   b) $3 \times 4 + 2.6$

   $=$

   $=$

   c) $3.1 \times (4 + 2)$

   $=$

   $=$

   d) $0.5 \times 4 + \dfrac{1}{2} \times 4$

   $=$

   $=$

   e) $2 \times 2 \times 2 \div 4$

   $=$

   $=$

   f) $2.5 \times 4 + 4.6$

   $=$

   $=$

2. Verify that the equation is true.

   a) $(2 + 5) \times 3.1 \quad = \quad 2 \times 3.1 + 5 \times 3.1$

   $(2 + 5) \times 3.1 \quad$ and $\quad 2 \times 3.1 + 5 \times 3.1$

   $= 7 \times 3.1 \qquad\qquad = 6.2 + 15.5$

   $= 21.7 \qquad\qquad\quad = 21.7$

   b) $2.1 \times (4 + 5) \quad = \quad 2.1 \times 4 + 2.1 \times 5$

   c) $3 + 14 \quad = \quad (3 + 4) + (14 - 4)$

   d) $0.5 \times 12 \quad = \quad (0.5 \times 10) + (0.5 \times 2)$

   e) $(7 \times 10) \div 5 \quad = \quad 7 \times (10 \div 5)$

   f) $(6 + 15) \div 3 \quad = \quad (6 \div 3) + (15 \div 3)$

> **REMINDER ▶** Powers are a short form for multiplication.
>
> Examples: $5^3 = 5 \times 5 \times 5 = 25 \times 5 = 125$, and $\left(\dfrac{1}{3}\right)^2 = \dfrac{1}{3} \times \dfrac{1}{3} = \dfrac{1 \times 1}{3 \times 3} = \dfrac{1}{9}$

3. Calculate the expression.

   a) $2^3 = 2 \times 2 \times 2 = 8$

   b) $3^2 + 1 =$

   c) $\left(\dfrac{1}{4}\right)^2 =$

   d) $4^2 + 3 \times 0.2 =$

   e) $4 \times \left(\dfrac{1}{2}\right)^3 =$

   f) $7 - 9 \times \left(\dfrac{1}{3}\right)^2 =$

   g) $2^3 \div 4 =$

   BONUS ▶ $2 \times 0.3^2 \div 6 =$

When replacing a variable with a number, we use brackets.

Example: Replacing n with $\frac{1}{2}$ in the expression $3n$ gives $3\left(\frac{1}{2}\right)$, which is another way to write $3 \times \frac{1}{2}$.

4. Replace the variable with the given number, and then evaluate.

a) $3x + \frac{5}{8}$, $x = \frac{1}{8}$

$3\left(\frac{1}{8}\right) + \frac{5}{8}$

$= \frac{3}{8} + \frac{5}{8}$

$= \frac{8}{8} = 1$

b) $5n - \frac{2}{3}$, $n = \frac{1}{3}$

c) $3m^2$, $m = 5$

d) s^3, $s = \frac{1}{2}$

$\left(\frac{1}{2}\right)^3$

$= \frac{1}{2} \times \frac{1}{2} \times \frac{1}{2}$

$= \frac{1}{8}$

e) $6z^2$, $z = \frac{1}{3}$

f) $4t^3 + 1$, $t = \frac{1}{4}$

g) $n^2 - \frac{1}{25}$, $n = \frac{2}{5}$

h) $3\frac{1}{4} - 3n$, $n = \frac{1}{4}$

REMINDER ▶ The area of a square with sides s is $A = s \times s$.

In power form, the area is $A = s^2$. For example, the area of a square with sides $s = \frac{1}{5}$ m is

$$\left(\frac{1}{5}\right)^2 = \frac{1}{5} \times \frac{1}{5} = \frac{1 \times 1}{5 \times 5} = \frac{1}{25} \text{ m}^2.$$

5. Find the area of the square with the given side length.

a) $s = 3$ cm

$A = 3 \text{ cm} \times 3 \text{ cm}$

$A = 9 \text{ cm}^2$

b) $s = \frac{1}{2}$ ft

$A =$

$A =$

c) $s = 2.5$ in

$A =$

$A =$

d) $s = 1\frac{1}{4}$ yd

$A =$

$A =$

EE6-14 Multiplication Equations and Word Problems

Smaller part: ☐

Larger part: ☐☐☐

The larger part is 3 times the size of the smaller part.

The scale factor is 3.

You can write an equation to find one part from the other:

Larger part = scale factor × smaller part

1. Circle the larger thing or quantity. Underline the smaller thing or quantity.

   a) A (high rise) is four times taller than a house.

   b) There are five times as many apples as pears.

   c) There are four times as many cats as dogs.

   d) Ed's bag is five times lighter than his suitcase.

   e) A mouse is four times smaller than a cat.

   f) A bus holds ten times as many people as a car.

2. Fill in the blanks. Use x for the unknown amount.

   a) Maya has 6 times as many stamps as Dan. Maya has 24 stamps. How many stamps does Dan have?

   Larger amount: _number of Maya's stamps_ ☐24☐   Smaller amount: _number of Dan's stamps_ ☐x☐

   Equation: $\underset{\text{Larger part}}{\underline{\quad x \quad}} = \underset{\text{Scale factor}}{\underline{\quad 6 \quad}} \times \underset{\text{Smaller part}}{\underline{\quad 24 \quad}}$

   b) A cherry is 10 times lighter than an apple. An apple weighs 30 grams. How much does the cherry weigh?

   Larger amount: _____ ☐   Smaller amount: _____ ☐

   Equation: $\underset{\text{Larger part}}{\underline{\qquad}} = \underset{\text{Scale factor}}{\underline{\qquad}} \times \underset{\text{Smaller part}}{\underline{\qquad}}$

   c) A CD player costs $225. A computer costs three times as much. How much does the computer cost?

   d) Lara is 4 times older than Neil. Lara is 12 years old. How old is Neil?

3. Write and solve an equation for the problem.

   a) Carl planted 8 times as many tomato plants as rose bushes. He planted 32 rose bushes. How many tomato plants did Carl plant?

   b) A whale shark is five times longer than a great white shark. A whale shark is 20 meters long. How long is a great white shark?

   c) A chair is four times lighter than a table. The table weighs 220 kg. How much does the chair weigh?

   d) A female Nile crocodile weighs 840 pounds, 4 times as much as a female American alligator. How much does the female American alligator weigh?

4. Fill in the chart. Use *x* for the unknown.

		Total Number of Things	Number of Sets	Number in Each Set	Equation
a)	40 pictures 8 pictures on each page	40	*x*	8	40 = 8x
b)	30 people 5 vans				
c)	24 flowers 6 pots				
d)	4 chairs at each table 11 tables				
e)	50 houses 10 houses on each block				
f)	9 boxes 22 pencils in each box				

5. Solve each equation in Question 4.

6. Write and solve an equation for the problem.

a) A train has 10 cars and 1,960 seats. How many seats are in each car?

b) A parking lot has 12 rows and 492 parking spots. How many cars can park in each row?

c) A maple tree is 10 m tall. A pine tree is 3 times taller. How tall is the pine tree?

d) A board game costs 3 times as much as a soft toy. The board game costs $19.50. How much does the soft toy cost?

e) Darya is twice as old as Diba. Darya is 13 years old. How old is Diba?

7. Solve these multistep problems.

a) Jane has 7 stickers. Mark has 5 times as many stickers as Jane. How many stickers do they have altogether?

b) There are 4 times as many people in City A as in City B. There are 257,301 people in City B. How many people are in City A?

c) The planet Uranus is about 1,780 million miles from the Sun. Uranus is twice as far from the Sun as the planet Saturn.

i) How far from the Sun is Saturn?

ii) How far is Uranus from Saturn?

EE6-15 More Multistep Word Problems

1. Fill in the table.

Problem	Parts	How Many?	Scale Factor / Difference
a) 4 people can ride in a car. 100 times as many people can ride in a train.	Number of people in a car	4	Scale factor: _100_
	Number of people in train	x	Difference: ~~~~
b) There are 30 fish in a tank. There are four times as many snails.			Scale factor: _____
			Difference: _____
c) A bed is 55 cm shorter than a desk. The desk is 115 cm long.			Scale factor: _____
			Difference: _____
d) A bike costs $60 more than a skateboard. The bike costs $240.			Scale factor: _____
			Difference: _____

2. Calculate the total for each problem in Question 1. If you do not know the difference, calculate it too.

3. Jack is 3 times older than Raj. Saul is 4 years older than Raj. Raj is $7\frac{1}{2}$ years old.

   a) How old is Jack?

   b) How old is Saul?

4. Ivan bought 8 jazz CDs and 6 rock CDs. Each CD costs $6.50.

   a) How many CDs did Ivan buy altogether?

   b) How much did the CDs cost?

5. Avi earns $9.25 per hour. She worked 4 hours on Monday, 5 hours on Wednesday, and 2 hours on Friday.

   a) How many hours did Avi work in the week?

   b) Did Avi earn $100 in the week?

6. Ms. Sinha's class has twice as many boys as girls. There are 18 boys in the class.

   a) How many girls are in the class?

   b) How many students are in the class?

   c) How many more boys than girls are in the class?

7. Kevin is 400 km from home on Friday morning. He cycles 65 km toward home each day. Will he be halfway home by Sunday evening?

8. Which question do you need to ask before you will be able to solve the problem?

 a) Malia has twice as many hockey cards as Rich does. Malia has 10 more hockey cards than Henry. Henry has 16 cards. How many cards does Rich have?

 How many cards does Malia have? _____

 b) Blake is twice as old as Miki. Miki is 3 years older than Nadia. Nadia is 5 years old. How old is Blake?

 _____

 c) Marcus is 4 years younger than Avon. Avon is 3 times as old as Sara. Sara is 2 years old. How old is Marcus?

 _____

 d) Rani had $73. She spent $15 for three hats, $8 on a scarf, and $12 on a pair of mitts. How much money does Rani have left?

 _____

9. Remi has 3 times as many baseball cards as Mary. Mary has 5 times as many baseball cards as Joe. Joe has 2 baseball cards. How many does Remi have?

10. Joel is 3 times older than Nina. Nina is 4 years older than Kahn. Kahn is 2 years old. How old are Joel and Nina?

11. Mrs. Kerr bought 3 packs of 12 blue pens. She also bought 5 red pens.

 a) How many pens did she buy altogether?

 b) Each pack of blue pens costs $7.50, and each red pen costs $1. How much did she pay for the pens?

12. The longest side of a triangle is 5 times as long as the shortest side. The shortest side is 12.5 cm. The other side is 7.3 cm shorter than the longest side. What are the lengths of the two unknown sides of the triangle?

13. Mona's basket holds 24 apples and Ava's basket holds 30 apples. They each collected less than 150 apples. How many baskets did they collect if they collected the same number of apples?

14. Carmen bought a bike lock for $32 and two bike lights for $12 each. After making these purchases, he had $15 left. How much money did he have to start with?

NS6-63 Opposite Values

1. Ron is playing a board game with a friend. During the game, they gain and lose play money.

   Write + before the amount to show a gain and − to show a loss.

   a) a gain of $3   b) a loss of $5   c) a loss of $8   d) a gain of $7

   ___+ $3___   _____   _____   _____

   Opposite values cancel each other out. The result is no gain and no loss.
   Example: A gain of $4 cancels out a loss of $4.

   You can use integers to represent opposite values.
   Example: +4 cancels out −4.

   ---

2. Write the integer that represents the gain or the loss.

   a) a gain of 4¢   b) a loss of 7¢   c) a gain of 50¢   d) a loss of 62¢

   ___+ 4___   _____   _____   _____

   e) a gain of 15¢   f) a loss of 30¢   g) a loss of 33¢   h) a gain of 74¢

   _____

3. Circle the better result.

   a) gained $4   b) lost $4   c) gained $2   d) gained $3

      gained $7   lost $7   lost $5   lost $2

   e) lost $30   f) lost $82   g) gained $38   h) gained $65

      lost $20   gained $41   lost $35   gained $49

4. a) Show the gains and losses on the number line.

   A. a gain of $3   **B.** A loss of $4   **C.** A gain of $6   **D.** A loss of $5

   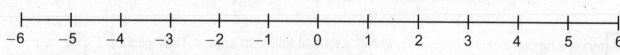

   b) Order your answers from worst result to best result. _____ , _____ , _____ , _____

   How does the number line show you the order? _____

   _____

Protons and electrons have an electric charge.
A proton has a charge of +1.

⊕

3 protons have a charge of +3.

⊕ ⊕ ⊕

An electron has a charge of −1.

⊖

4 electrons have a charge of −4.

⊖ ⊖ ⊖ ⊖

---

5. Describe the total electric charge as an integer.

a) ⊕ ⊕   b) ⊖ ⊖ ⊖   c) ⊕ ⊕ ⊕ ⊕ ⊕ ⊕ ⊕

_____   _____   _____

6. Draw a picture to show how many electrons (−) or protons (+) would have
the given charge.

a) −5   b) +4

⊖ ⊖ ⊖ ⊖ ⊖

c) +2   d) −3

Protons and electrons have electric charges that cancel each other out. When an object has the same
number of protons and electrons, it has no electric charge.

---

7. Write the electric charge. Hint: Circle the amounts that cancel each other out.

a) ⊕ ⊕ ⊖
   ⊖ ⊖ ⊖   ___−2___

b) ⊕ ⊖ ⊖ ⊕ ⊖ ⊖
   ⊖ ⊖ ⊖ ⊕ ⊖ ⊕   _____

c) ⊖ ⊕ ⊕ ⊕ ⊖
   ⊕ ⊖ ⊖ ⊕ ⊖   _____

d) ⊕ ⊖ ⊖ ⊖ ⊕ ⊖
   ⊕ ⊖ ⊕ ⊕ ⊕ ⊕   _____

e) ⊕ ⊕ ⊖
   ⊖ ⊖ ⊕   _____

f) ⊖ ⊖ ⊖ ⊖ ⊕
   ⊕ ⊕ ⊕ ⊕ ⊖   _____

8. What does an electric charge of 0 mean? _____

_____

NS6-64 Debits, Credits, and Debt

A bank statement shows a **credit** when you add money to your bank account. It shows a **debit** when you take money out of your bank account.

The **balance** is the total amount of money in the account. The bank statement below shows two credits and no debits. You can use a number line to find the balance.

Debit	Credit	Balance
	$4	*$4*
	$3	*$7*

What is $4 + $3?

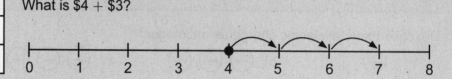

1. Use the number line to complete the balance column.

a)

Debit	Credit	Balance
	$8	*$8*
$5		

What is $8 − $5?

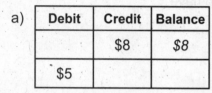

A bank account balance can be negative!

b)

Debit	Credit	Balance
	$3	*$3*
$5		−$2

What is $3 − $5?

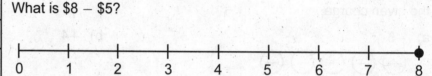

c)

Debit	Credit	Balance
	$2	
$3		

What is _____?

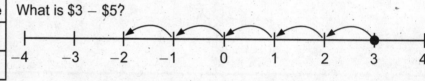

d)

Debit	Credit	Balance
	$4	
$6		

What is _____?

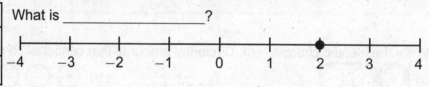

e)

Debit	Credit	Balance
	$1	
	$3	

What is _____?

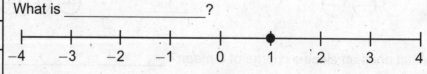

2. Four people have money in their bank accounts.

Ari. −$3   **Bob.** +$4   **Chen.** −$6   **Dave.** +$5

  a) Whose bank account would you most like to have? _____

  b) Whose bank account would you least like to have? _____

  c) Show each person's balance on the number line.

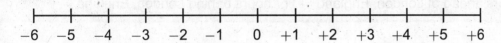

     −6   −5   −4   −3   −2   −1   0   +1   +2   +3   +4   +5   +6

  d) Write the four names in order from least balance to greatest balance.

    _____ < _____ < _____ < _____

3. Circle the account balance that is greater.

  a) (−$30)   −$40   b) −$12   +$3   c) +$6   +$30   d) +$4   −$5

> If your bank account is −$10, you have a **debt** of $10. A debt becomes **greater** when more money is owed.

4. Circle the account balance that shows the greater debt.

  a) (−$5)   −$4   b) −$12   −$15   c) −$6   −$30   d) −$8   −$20

5. Complete the chart.

		Whose debt is greater?	Whose bank account balance is greater?
a)	Sarah's debt is $12. Ravi's debt is $15.		
b)	Sarah's bank account is −$50. Ravi's bank account is −$30.		
c)	Sarah's debt is $42. Ravi's debt is $33.		
d)	Sarah's bank account is −$27. Ravi's bank account is −$28.		

6. Write "greater" or "smaller."

A greater amount owing means the bank account has a _____ amount.

7. What is better, a debt of $10 or a debt of $20? Explain.

NS6-65 The Meaning of Zero

Integers can be used to describe opposite directions from a chosen point. The chosen point becomes the 0. Examples:

• Temperature: degrees warmer than 0°F (+) or degrees colder than 0°F (−)

• Elevation: feet higher than sea level (+) or feet lower than sea level (−)

• Time zones: hours ahead of London, England (+) or hours behind London, England (−)

1. What does each integer represent in the context?

a) +3 (temperature)   _____*3 degrees warmer than 0°F*_____

b) −4 (temperature)   _____

c) +2 (elevation)   _____

d) −5 (time zone)   _____

e) +3 (time zone)   _____

f) 0 (elevation)   _____

g) 0 (time zone)   _____

People often use two different temperature scales, Celsius (°C) and Fahrenheit (°F), with different temperatures set as 0.

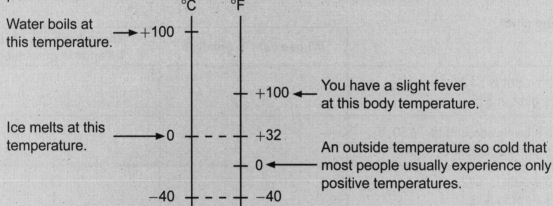

2. At what temperature in degrees Fahrenheit does ice melt? _____ °F

3. At what temperature are the two scales the same? _____ °C or °F

4. Rowan said, "I went skating when the temperature was 0°, so the ice was soft."
   Do you think she meant 0°C or 0°F? Explain.

> **REMINDER** ▶ Integers can be used to describe opposite values that cancel each other out.
>
> Examples:
> Bank account: more credits than debits (+) or more debits than credits (−)
> Electric charge: more protons than electrons (+) or more electrons than protons (−)
> +/− rating: more points for than against (+) or more points against than for (−)

5. Which integer represents the amount?

a) Niveah put $5 more into her account than she took out. _____

b) Jeremy took out of his account $7 more than he put in. _____

c) Bilal put into his account the same amount as he took out. _____

d) An object has 4 more electrons than protons. _____

e) An object has 8 more protons than electrons. _____

f) An object has 8 fewer protons than electrons. _____

g) An object has the same number of protons as electrons. _____

h) Lucy's team had 4 more points for them than against them. _____

i) Hareel's team had 3 fewer points for them than against them. _____

j) Jamal's team had the same number of points for as against. _____

6. Does the situation show an electric charge of 0?

a) 3 protons and 3 electrons _____   b) 0 electrons and 0 protons _____

c) 5 electrons and 4 protons _____   d) 8 electrons and 8 protons _____

7. What does each integer represent in the context?

a) +3 (bank account) _____

b) −4 (bank account) _____

c) 0 (bank account) _____

d) +2 (electric charge) _____

e) −1 (electric charge) _____

f) 0 (electric charge) _____

NS6-66 Opposite Integers Again

1. Find the distance from 0.

   a)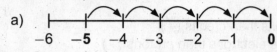

   −5 is ___5___ units from 0.

   b)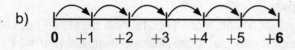

   +6 is _____ units from 0.

   c)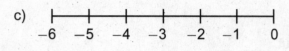

   −6 is _____ units from 0.

   d)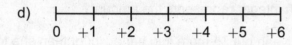

   +3 is _____ units from 0.

   e)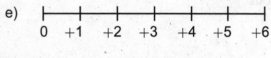

   +5 is _____ units from 0.

   f)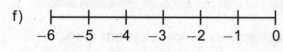

   −3 is _____ units from 0.

REMINDER ▶ Opposite integers are the same distance from 0, but in opposite directions.

---

2. Write the opposite integer. Hint: Look at your answers to Question 1.

   a) +3 _____   b) −5 _____   c) +6 _____   **BONUS ▶** −183 _____

3. The opposite of +5 is −5. What is the opposite of −5? _____

4. a) What is the opposite of −13? _____

   b) What is the opposite integer to your answer in part a)? _____

5. The opposite of +4 is _____. The opposite of the opposite of +4 is _____.

   BONUS ▶ What is the opposite of the opposite of −183? _____

6. a) Write the integers that represent the amounts that cancel.

   i) 3 protons and 3 electrons

   _____ and _____

   ii) a debit of $2 and a credit of $2

   _____ and _____

   iii) 4 electrons and _____ protons

   iv) a credit of $7 and a _____ of $7

   b) Look at your answers to part a). What do you notice about the integers that represent amounts that cancel?

NS6-67 Distance Apart

1. How far from 0 is the integer?

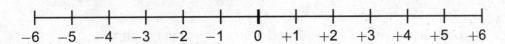

a) −4   b) +5   c) −6   d) +3

___4___ units   _____ units   _____ units   _____ units

2. How far apart are the integers? Hint: Add the distances from 0.

a)

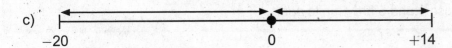

___4___ + ___5___ = _____, so −4 and +5 are _____ units apart.

b)

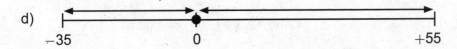

_____ + _____ = _____, so −3 and +4 are _____ units apart.

c)

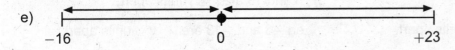

_____ + _____ = _____, so −20 and +14 are _____ units apart.

d)

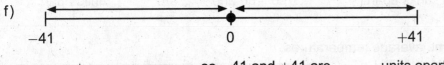

_____ + _____ = _____, so −35 and +55 are _____ units apart.

e)

_____ + _____ = _____, so −16 and +23 are _____ units apart.

f)

_____ + _____ = _____, so −41 and +41 are _____ units apart.

g) −8 and +10 are _____ units apart.   h) −9 and + 7 are _____ units apart.

3. How far apart are the integers?

a)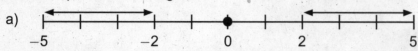

   −5 and −2 are _____ units apart.   2 and 5 are _____ units apart.

b)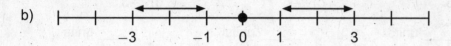

   −3 and −1 are _____ units apart.   1 and 3 are _____ units apart.

c)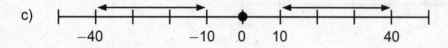

   −40 and −10 are _____ units apart.   10 and 40 are _____ units apart.

Remember: Opposite integers are the same distance from 0, but in opposite directions.

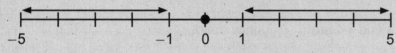

−5 and −1 are 4 units apart because 1 and 5 are 4 units apart.

---

4. Subtract to find the distance between the positive integers. Then write the distance between the negative integers.

a) ↙ 8 − 3

   3 and 8 are ☐ units apart,

   so −3 and −8 are _____ units apart.

b) ↙ 12 − 4

   4 and 12 are ☐ units apart,

   so −4 and −12 are _____ units apart.

c) 2 and 5 are ☐ units apart,

   so −2 and −5 are _____ units apart.

d) 3 and 13 are ☐ units apart,

   so −3 and −13 are _____ units apart.

e) 10 and 45 are ☐ units apart,

   so −10 and −45 are _____ units apart.

f) 60 and 42 are ☐ units apart,

   so −60 and −42 are _____ units apart.

BONUS ▶ The table shows some average temperatures.

Is the North Pole's winter temperature closer to its summer temperature or to the temperature on Mars?

North Pole in Summer	North Pole in Winter	Mars
+32°F	−30°F	−81°F

NS6-68 Absolute Value

The **absolute value** of a number is its distance from 0.

Examples: The absolute value of −3 is 3.

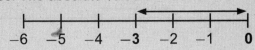

The absolute value of +4 is 4.

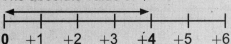

1. What is the absolute value?

a)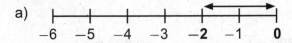

The absolute value of −2 is __2__.

b)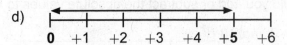

The absolute value of +3 is _____.

c)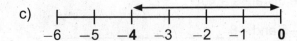

The absolute value of −4 is _____.

d)

The absolute value of +5 is _____.

2. Would you *add* or *subtract* the absolute values to find the distance apart?

a)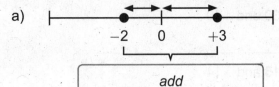

add

b)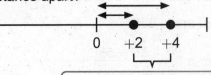

c)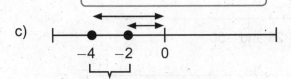

d)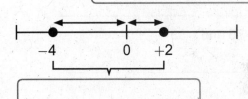

e)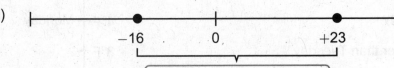

f)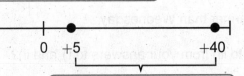

BONUS ▶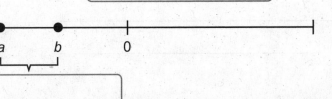

To find the distance between two numbers:

Add the absolute values of numbers on **opposite** sides of 0.

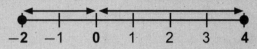

−2 and 4 are 2 + 4 = 6 units apart.

Subtract the absolute values of numbers on **the same** side of 0.

−5 and −3 are 5 − 3 = 2 units apart.

3. Circle the pairs of integers that are on the same side of 0.

   −2 and −3   −2 and +5   +4 and −5   +6 and +3

4. Would you add or subtract the absolute values to find the distance apart?

   a) −3 and −8 _____

   b) −5 and +8 _____

   c) +20 and −100 _____

   d) +32 and +45 _____

5. Write an addition or subtraction equation to find the distance between the integers.

   a) −20 and +35

   _____ 20 + 35 = 55 _____

   b) +30 and +50

   _____

   c) +12 and −40

   _____

   d) −15 and +14

   _____

   e) −75 and −35

   _____

   f) −25 and −50

   _____

6. a) The number line shows the temperatures for three different days.

   Write how much warmer each day is.

   i) Monday was _____°F warmer than Tuesday.

   ii) Tuesday was _____°F warmer than Wednesday.

   iii) Monday was _____°F warmer than Wednesday.

   b) How can you get the answer to iii) from your answers to i) and ii)?

   _____

   _____

   _____

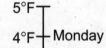

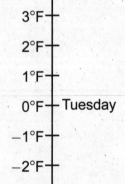

NS6-69 Concepts in Absolute Value

The notation $|-3|$ is short for "the absolute value of -3." Examples: $|-3| = 3$ and $|+8| = 8$.

1. Write the absolute value.

   a) $|-4| = $ _____   b) $|+6| = $ _____   c) $|-18| = $ _____   d) $|+14| = $ _____

   e) $|-7\frac{1}{2}| = $ _____   f) $|-3.4| = $ _____   g) $|+8\frac{3}{5}| = $ _____   h) $|-12.46| = $ _____

2. Write the numbers in order. Hint: Look at your answers to Question 1.

   $|-4|$ $|+6|$ $|-18|$ $|+14|$ _____ < _____ < _____ < _____

3. a) Complete the table. Remember: 1 m = 100 cm.

	Distance from Sea Level	What is closer to sea level, the bird or the fish?	How much higher than the fish is the bird?
i)	The bird is at $+300$ m. The fish is at -100 m.		
ii)	The bird is at $+35.6$ m. The fish is at -41.2 m.		
iii)	The bird is at $+30$ m. The fish is at -87 cm.		
iv)	The bird is at $+5$ m. The fish is at -641 cm.		

   b) How did you use the absolute values to determine which animal is closer to sea level?

   Did you add them, subtract them, or compare them? _____

   c) How did you use the absolute values to determine how much higher the bird is than the fish?

   Did you add them, subtract them, or compare them? _____

4. Justify your answers using absolute value notation.

   a) How much colder than 0°F is -7°F?   _____ $|-7| = 7$, so 7°F _____

   b) Sarah's bank account has $-\$100$. What is the size of her debt? _____

   c) A fish is at -80 m. How far below sea level is the fish? _____

5. What is the absolute value of 0? Explain how you know.

6. Aliya says that opposite integers have the same absolute value. Is she right? Explain.

7. An early form of checkers was invented around 3000 BC. The modern form was invented around 1100 AD. How much later is that?

8. The earliest form of writing occurred around 3200 BC. The printing press was invented around 1440 AD. How much later is that?

9. The coldest temperature ever recorded on Earth was −129°F in Vostok, Antarctica. The warmest temperature ever recorded was +134°F in Death Valley, California.

How much warmer is the warmest temperature than the coldest?

10. How much better is a 14 yard gain in football than a 5 yard loss? Use integers to explain your answer.

11. A helicopter is flying 200 m above sea level. A fish is 100 m below sea level.

a) How much higher is the helicopter than the fish?

b) +200 is how much greater than −100?

12. A ball is dropped from 80 cm above the ground. It falls into a hole 25 cm below the ground. Using ground level as 0, draw an integer number line to show the situation.

How far did the ball drop in total?

13. a) Complete the table by finding the difference between the daily highs in January and July.

Place	Average Daily High in January	Average Daily High in July	Difference	Distance from Equator
Orlando, USA	22°C	33°C		3,172 km
Quito, Ecuador	19°C	19°C		24 km
Juneau, USA	−2°C	18°C		6,485 km
South Pole	−26°C	−56°C		10,002 km

b) The temperature difference between January and July generally increases as the city gets farther from the equator. Does this agree with your answers in part a)? _____

14. Cairo, Egypt, is 2 hours ahead of London, England. London is 5 hours
ahead of Boston, USA. How many hours ahead of Boston is Cairo? _____

15. Liam's time zone is 6 hours ahead of Kim's. It is 5:00 p.m. in Kim's time zone.
What time is it in Liam's time zone?

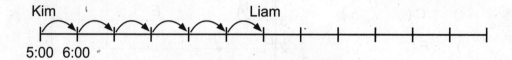

16. Bob lives in time zone +4. Jan is in time zone −3.

a) How many hours ahead of Jan is Bob? _____

b) Jan calls Bob at 3:00 p.m., Jan's time. What time is it, Bob's time?

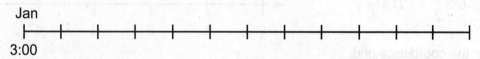

c) Jan tells Bob there is a figure skating event at 7:30 p.m, Jan's time.
At what time can Bob watch the event live on TV?

17. Use integers to represent locations north of the equator (positive) and south
of the equator (negative).

a) Jayden lives in a city that is 400 km north of the equator. His location is at _____ km.

b) Alice lives in a city 2,300 km south of the equator. Her location is at _____ km.

c) Who lives closer to the equator? Did you compare the **values** of the integers
or the **absolute values**?

d) Who lives farther north than the other person? Did you compare the **values**
of the integers or the **absolute values**?

e) Who do you expect to live in a warmer climate? Explain.

18. a) How far apart are the integers?

    i) −1 and 1   ii) −2 and 2   iii) −3 and 3   iv) −4 and 4   **BONUS ▶** −300 and 300

b) How can you get the distance between an integer and its opposite if you know the
absolute value of the integer?

G6-20 The Four Quadrants of a Coordinate Grid

REMINDER ▶ Two numbers in order in brackets are called an ordered pair.
An ordered pair defines a point on a coordinate grid.
The point (0, 0) is called the origin.

A (4, 1)   B (1, 4)

x-coordinate   y-coordinate   *x-coordinate   y-coordinate*

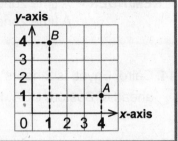

1. Fill in the coordinates for the given points.

   A (_1_ , _3_)   B (__ , __)   C (__ , __)

   D (__ , __)   E (__ , __)   F (__ , __)

   G (__ , __)   H (__ , __)   I (__ , __)

   J (__ , __)   K (__ , __)   L (__ , __)

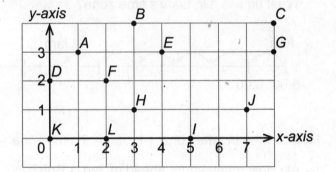

2. a) Mark the points on the number line.

   A 1.5   B 0.5   C 3$\frac{1}{2}$ D 4$\frac{1}{4}$

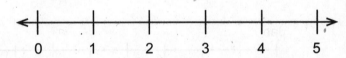

   b) Mark the points on the coordinate grid.

   A (0.5, 1.5)   B (2.5, 1)   C (4, 1.5)

   D (5.5, 0.5)   E (1$\frac{1}{2}$, 2)   F (7, $\frac{1}{2}$)

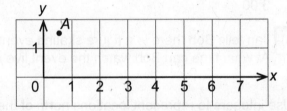

You can extend a grid to include negative numbers.
The **axes** are perpendicular lines that divide the grid
into four parts. These parts are called **quadrants**.

We use Roman numerals to number the quadrants.

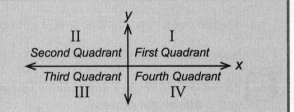

3. a) Label the origin (*O*), the *x*-axis, and the *y*-axis.

   b) Label the axes with positive and negative integers.

   c) Number the four quadrants (I, II, III, IV).

   d) Which quadrants are these points in?

   A (2, 2) __*I*__   B (−2, −2) _____

   C (−2, 2) _____   D (2, −2) _____

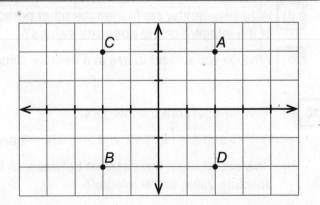

4. In Figure 1, point A (2, 3) is in the first quadrant.
Its x- and y-coordinates are both **positive**.

a) Find the coordinates of the points.

P (,   ) Q (,   )

R (,   ) S (,   )

b) Plot and label.

B (3, 2) C (1, 4) D (2, 6)

5. In Figure 1, point F (−2, 3) is in the second
quadrant. Its x-coordinate is **negative** and
its y-coordinate is **positive**.

a) Find the coordinates of the points.

K (,   ) L (,   )

M (,   ) N (,   )

b) Plot and label.

G (−3, 2) H (−2, 6) I (−4, 3)

6. In Figure 2, point A (−2, −3) is in the third quadrant.
Its x- and y-coordinates are both **negative**.

a) Find the coordinates of the points.

K (,   ) L (,   )

M (,   ) N (,   )

b) Plot and label.

B (−3, −4) C (−2, −6) D (−4, −3)

7. In Figure 2, point F (2, −3) is in the fourth
quadrant. Its x-coordinate is **positive** and
its y-coordinate is **negative**.

a) Find the coordinates of the points.

P (,   ) Q (,   )

R (,   ) S (,   )

b) Plot and label.

G (3, −4) H (1, −6)

I (4, −1) J (4, −6)

Figure 1

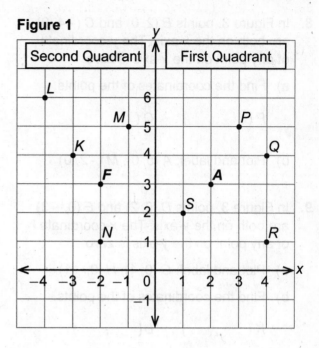

Figure 2

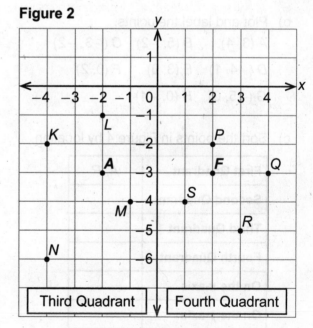

8. In Figure 3, points B (2, 0) and C (−4, 0) are both on the x-axis. The y-coordinate of any point on the x-axis is **zero**.

a) Find the coordinates of the points.

P (,   )   Q (,   )

b) Plot and label: A (5, 0), M (−2, 0)

9. In Figure 3, points D (0, 2) and E (0, −3) are both on the y-axis. The x-coordinate of any point on the y-axis is **zero**.

a) Plot and label: G (0, 4), H (0, −1).

b) Find the coordinates of the points.

K (,   )   L (,   )

Figure 3

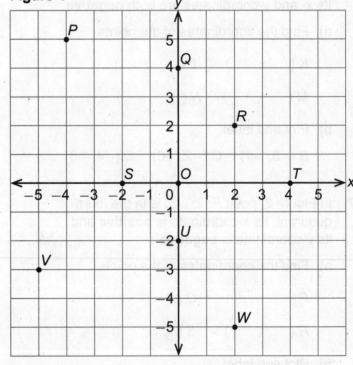

10. a) Find the coordinates of the points in Figure 4.

O (,   ) P (,   ) Q (,   ) R (,   ) S (,   )

T (,   ) U (,   ) V (,   ) W (,   )

b) Plot and label the points.

A (3, 4)   B (5, −2)   C (−3, −2)

D (−4, 1)   E (3, 0)   F (0, 2)

G (−5, 0)   H (0, −4)

c) Sort the points in Figure 4 by location.

First Quadrant	A, R
Second Quadrant	
Third Quadrant	
Fourth Quadrant	
On the x-axis	
On the y-axis	
At the Origin	

Figure 4

11. Which quadrant is each point in?

a) (−732, 805) _____   b) (732, −805) _____   c) (−732, −805) _____   d) (732, 805) _____

G6-21 Coordinate Systems

1. Mark the points on the number line.

   A 1.4 B −0.6 $C \dfrac{1}{2}$ D −1$\dfrac{2}{5}$ E −2.1 F 3$\dfrac{2}{10}$

2. a) Find the coordinates of the points in Figure 1.   **Figure 1**

   A ($-4\dfrac{1}{2}$, $1\dfrac{1}{2}$) B (,   )

   C (,   ) D (,   )

   E (,   ) F (,   )

   G (,   ) H (,   )

   b) Plot and label the points.

   I (4, 2) J (3, −1)

   K $\left(-1\dfrac{1}{2}, -1\right)$ L $\left(-2, \dfrac{1}{2}\right)$ M $\left(1\dfrac{1}{2}, 0\right)$

   N $\left(0, 3\dfrac{1}{2}\right)$ O $\left(-2\dfrac{1}{2}, -4\dfrac{1}{2}\right)$ P $\left(-3\dfrac{1}{2}, 2\dfrac{1}{2}\right)$

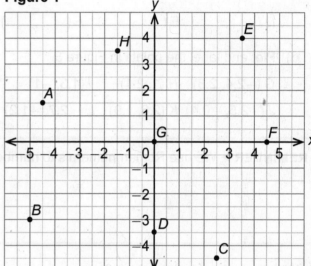

3. a) Draw lines parallel to the axes to find the coordinates of the points in Figure 2.   **Figure 2**

   A ($1\dfrac{1}{2}$, $-1\dfrac{1}{4}$) B (,   )

   C (,   ) D (,   )

   E (,   ) F (,   )

   b) Plot and label the points.

   G $\left(3\dfrac{1}{4}, 0\right)$ H $\left(0, -1\dfrac{3}{4}\right)$

   I $\left(-2\dfrac{3}{4}, 2\right)$ J $\left(3, -2\dfrac{1}{4}\right)$

   K $\left(-2\dfrac{1}{2}, -2\dfrac{1}{2}\right)$ L $\left(-1\dfrac{1}{2}, 2\dfrac{1}{2}\right)$

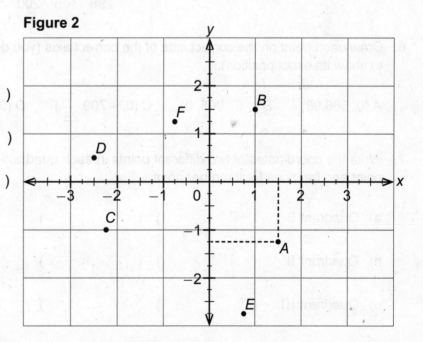

4. a) 2.7 cm = _____ mm 1.3 cm = _____ mm

b) Use a millimeter ruler to mark the points on the number line.

  P 2.7   *Q* −1.3

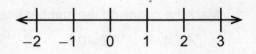

c) Draw lines parallel to the axes and measure
the distance using a millimeter ruler to find the
coordinates of the points in Figure 3.

  A (0.2, −1.3) *B* (,   ) *C* (,   )

  D (,   ) *E* (,   ) *F* (,   )

Figure 3

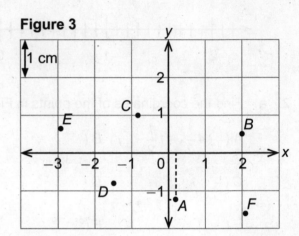

d) Plot and label the points in Figure 3.

  G (−2.4, 2.8) *H* (1, 2.1)   *I* (1.3, −1)

  J (−2.5, −0.4) *K* (2.6, 1.9) *L* (−2.7, −1.2)

REMINDER ▶ We use Roman numerals to number quadrants.

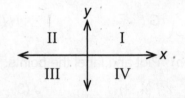

---

5. Which quadrant is the point in?

a) (−73.12, 80.5) _*II*_

b) (7.82, −8.55) _____

c) (−7.903, −.805) _____

d) (54.9, 435.98) _____

e) $(432\frac{167}{298}, -782\frac{91}{200})$ _____

f) $(-782\frac{91}{200}, 432\frac{167}{298})$ _____

6. Draw each point on the correct side of the correct axis (you don't have
to show its exact position).

  A (0, 566.98)   *B* (−67.905, 0)   *C* $(0, -709\frac{1}{28})$ *D* $(90\frac{16}{29}, 0)$

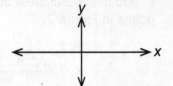

7. Write the coordinates of two different points in each quadrant. Use decimals for one
point and fractions for the other point.

a) Quadrant I: (,   ) (,   )

b) Quadrant II: (,   ) (,   )

c) Quadrant III: (,   ) (,   )

d) Quadrant IV :   (,   ) (,   )

G6-22 Horizontal and Vertical Lines

1. Plot the set of points on the coordinate system in Figure 1.
   Join the points with a line. Which axis is the line parallel to?

   a) (2, −2) (2, −1) (2, 0) (2, 1) (2, 2): ____-axis

   b) (−3, −3) (−3, −2) (−3, 0) (−3, 2): ____-axis

   c) (−4, 2) (−3, 2) (0, 2) (3, 2) (4, 2): ____-axis

Figure 1

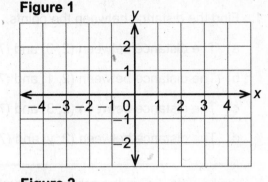

2. Plot the points P (3, 2) and Q (3, −1) in Figure 2.
   Draw the line PQ.

   a) Is the line you drew horizontal or vertical? _____

   Extend the line and draw three more points on it.

   Write the coordinates of each point:

   (,   ) (,   ) (,   )

   Compare the coordinates. What do all points on line PQ
   have in common?

   _____

Figure 2

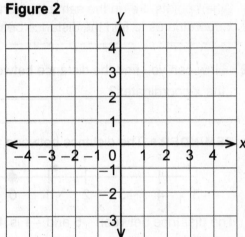

   b) Sort the points into the table.

   A (−12, −1)   B (−42, 71)   C (3, 142)   D (3, −14.2)

Not on the line PQ	On the line PQ, above P	On the line PQ, below Q

   c) Add another point to each column of the table in part b).

3. Plot the points P (3, 1) and R (−2, 1) in Figure 3.
   Draw the line PR.

   a) Is the line you drew horizontal or vertical? _____

   Extend the line and draw three more points on it.

   Write the coordinates of each point:

   (,   ) (,   ) (,   )

   Compare the coordinates. What do all points on line PR
   have in common?

   _____

Figure 3

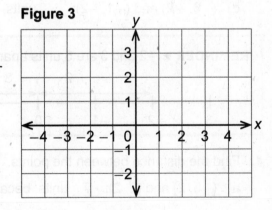

   b) Sort the points into the table.

   A (−12 $\frac{3}{8}$,1)   B (−902, 374)   C (367, 1)   D (−142, 1)

Not on the line PR	On the line PR, to the left of R	On the line PR, to the right of P

G6-23 Distance on Horizontal and Vertical Lines

1. Find the distance between the points.

   a) The distance between (2, 0) and (7, 0) is __5__ units.

   b) The distance between (2, 1) and (7, 1) is ____ units.

   c) The distance between (2, 3) and (7, 3) is ____ units.

   d) The distance between (2, y) and (7, y) is ____ units.

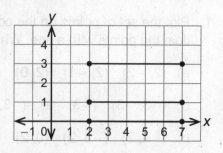

When points are on the same horizontal line, they have the same y-coordinates. You can use the x-coordinates to find the distance between the points.

2. How can you find the distance between the points in Question 1 using the x-coordinates? _____

REMINDER ▶ The distance between −5 and −1 is the same as the distance between 5 and 1.

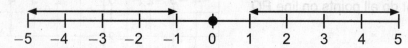

The distance between −5 and −1 is 4 units, because 5 − 1 = 4.

3. Find the distance between the points.

   a) (−7, 2) and (−4, 2): __3__ units, because ____$7 - 4 = 3$____

   b) (−6, 1) and (−3, 1): ____ units, because _____

   c) (−7, −1) and (−3, −1): ____ units, because _____

   d) (−6, −2) and (−1, −2): ____ units, because _____

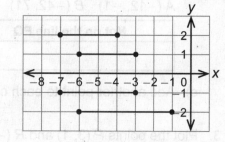

REMINDER ▶ −2 and 3 are 5 units apart, because 2 + 3 = 5.

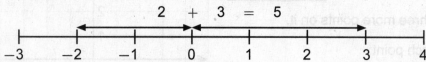

$$2 + 3 = 5$$

4. Find the distance between the points.

   a) (−5, 2) and (2, 2): __7__ units, because ____$5 + 2 = 7$____

   b) (−5, 1) and (2, 1): ____ units, because _____

   c) (−5, −1) and (2, −1): ____ units, because _____

   d) (−4, −2) and (1, −2): ____ units, because _____

   e) (−1, −3) and (3, −3): ____ units, because _____

   f) (−7, −4) and (2, −4): ____ units, because _____

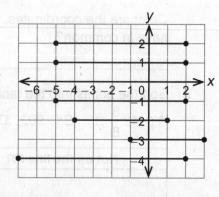

REMINDER ▶ The **absolute value** of a number is its distance from 0.
The absolute value of -3 is $|-3| = 3$.

To find the distance between two numbers:

Add the absolute values of numbers on **opposite** sides of 0.

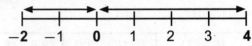

-2 and 4 are $2 + 4 = 6$ units apart.

Subtract the absolute values of numbers on **the same** side of 0.

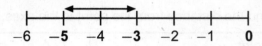

-5 and -3 are $5 - 3 = 2$ units apart.

5. Add or subtract the absolute values of the *x*-coordinates to find the distance between the points. Then plot the points on the grid and check your answer.

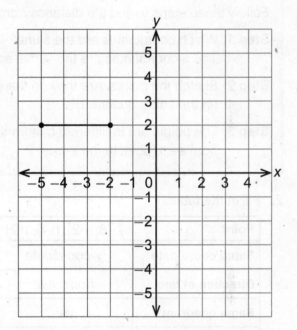

a) The distance between $(-5, 2)$ and $(-2, 2)$ is

    $\underline{\quad |-5| - |-2| \quad} = \underline{\quad 5 - 2 \quad} = \underline{\quad 3 \quad}$ units.

b) The distance between $(4, 4)$ and $(-2, 4)$ is

    $\underline{\qquad\qquad} = \underline{\qquad} = \underline{\quad}$ units.

c) The distance between $(-1, -5)$ and $(1, -5)$ is

    $\underline{\qquad\qquad} = \underline{\qquad} = \underline{\quad}$ units.

d) The distance between $(-3, 0)$ and $(1, 0)$ is

    $\underline{\qquad\qquad} = \underline{\qquad} = \underline{\quad}$ units.

e) The distance between $(-1, 2)$ and $(1, 2)$ is

    $\underline{\qquad\qquad} = \underline{\qquad} = \underline{\quad}$ units.

f) The distance between $(-4, -2)$ and $(-2, -2)$ is

    $\underline{\qquad\qquad} = \underline{\qquad} = \underline{\quad}$ units.

6. Find the distance between the points using the diagram.

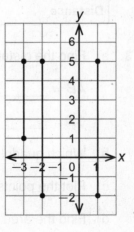

    a) $(-3, 1)$ and $(-3, 5)$: ____ units   b) $(1, -2)$ and $(1, 5)$: ____ units

    c) $(-2, -2)$ and $(-2, 5)$: ____ units   d) $(x, -2)$ and $(x, 5)$: ____ units

7. Add or subtract the absolute values of the *y*-coordinates to find the distance between the points.

    a) $(1, -3)$ and $(1, 2)$: ____ units   b) $(1, -5)$ and $(1, 2)$: ____ units

    c) $(-1, -2)$ and $(-1, 2)$: ____ units   d) $(-1, -5)$ and $(-1, -2)$: ____ units

    e) $(0, 2)$ and $(0, -3)$: ____ units   f) $(-3, -5)$ and $(-3, -12)$: ____ units

    g) $(184, -2)$ and $(184, 7)$: ____ units   h) $(-51, 2)$ and $(-51, -5)$: ____ units

G6-24 Using Distance to Identify Shapes

The distance from a point to the *x*-axis is the absolute value of the *y*-coordinate.

The distance from a point to the *y*-axis is the absolute value of the *x*-coordinate.

Example: Point (−3, 2) is 3 units from the *y*-axis and 2 units from the *x*-axis.

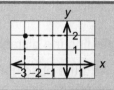

1. Find the distance from the point to the axes.

Point	(−4, 5)	(9, 5)	(6, −7)	(−15, −23)	(3.5, −8.12)
Distance to the *x*-axis	5				
Distance to the *y*-axis	4				

Follow these steps to find the distance from point *A* (−1, 2) to point *B* (−1, −1):

Step 1: Which coordinates are the same? Is the line *AB* horizontal or vertical?
The *x*-coordinates are the same, so the line *AB* is vertical.

Step 2: Sketch the points. Are they on the same side of the *x*-axis (in the same quadrant)?

Step 3: The points are in different quadrants, so add the distances from each point to the *x*-axis: 2 + 1 = 3.

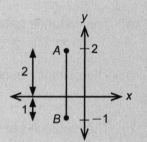

2. Fill in the table.

Point	(−8, −2), (−5, −2)	(8, 3), (8, 2)	(8, −3), (−6, −3)	(−5, 2), (−12, 2)
Same coordinate	*y*-coordinate			
Direction of line	horizontal			
Same quadrant?	yes			
Distance	8 − 5 = 3			

3. a) Find the distance between pairs of these points: *A* (−6, 4), *B* (1, 4), *C* (1, 2), *D* (−6, 2).

   AB = _____ = _____   *BC* = _____ = _____

   CD = _____ = _____   *AD* = _____ = _____

   b) Which quadrilateral do these points make? _____

   c) Plot the points on the grid to check your answer.

   d) Find the area of *ABCD* in square units. Area *ABCD* = _____

   e) Each square on the grid is $\frac{1}{4}$ inch long and $\frac{1}{4}$ inch wide.

   Find the area of *ABCD* in square inches. Area *ABCD* = _____

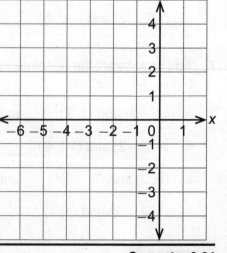

> **REMINDER** ▶ A quadrilateral with parallel sides can be a parallelogram or a trapezoid. If the parallel
> sides are equal, it is a parallelogram. If they are not equal, it is a trapezoid.

4. Which vertical or horizontal sides are parallel?

a) *A* (−6, 42), *B* (21, 30), *C* (21, 2), *D* (−6, −2)

_____ and _____

b) *E* (−1.2, −4.3), *F* (−1.5, 4), *G* (3.1, 4), *H* (2, −4.3)

_____ and _____

5. a) Which vertical or horizontal sides are parallel?

A (−2, 1), *B* (−2, 5), *C* (−5, 3), *D* (−5, −2)

_____ and _____

b) Find the lengths of the parallel sides.

_____ = _____ units   _____ = _____ units

c) Is *ABCD* a parallelogram or a trapezoid?

ABCD is a _____

d) Plot the points on the grid to check your answer.

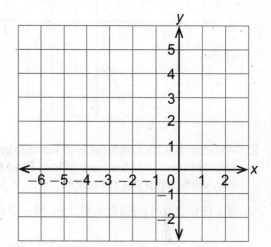

6. a) Which vertical or horizontal sides are parallel?

E (1, −2), *F* (−2, −2), *G* (0, 4), *H* (3, 4)

_____ and _____

b) Find the lengths of the parallel sides.

_____ = _____ units   _____ = _____ units

c) Is *EFGH* a parallelogram or a trapezoid?

EFGH is a _____

d) Plot the points on the grid to check your answer.

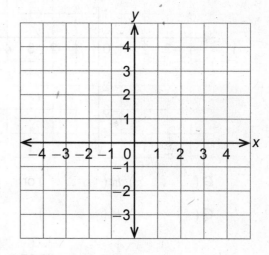

7. Identify the parallel sides of the quadrilateral. Find the length of each parallel side,
and then identify the quadrilateral.

a) *I* (−46, 42), *J* (54, 42),

K (21, 2), *L* (−26, 2)

b) *M* (−2, −1), *N* (−6, −3),

O $\left(-2\frac{1}{2}, -3\right)$, *P* $\left(1\frac{1}{2}, -1\right)$

c) *Q* (−0.6, 4.8), *R* (−0.6, −6.7),

S (−2.8, −6.7), *T* (−2.8, 4.8)

8. Remember: Area of triangle = base × height ÷ 2. The vertices of a triangle are
X (2.1, 3.4), *Y* (2.1, −3.8), *Z* (−4.8, −3.8). Find the area of the triangle.

BONUS ▶ Find the area of the quadrilateral in Question 7c).

G6-25 Quadrilaterals on Coordinate Grids

1. Predict the coordinates of the fourth vertex of a rectangle, and then plot the points on the grid to check your answer.

   a) $A(-3, 1), B(-3, -2), C(2, -2), D(\quad, \quad)$ b) $W(-5, 1), X(2, 1), Y(2, 4), Z(\quad, \quad)$

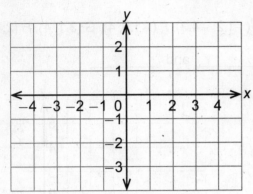 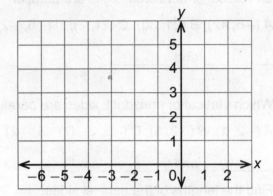

2. A rectangle has vertical and horizontal sides. One side length and the coordinates of two adjacent vertices are given. Find two possible sets of coordinates for the other two vertices of the rectangle:

   a) $E(-2, -1), F(1, -1)$, height = 2 units   b) $P(1, -1), Q(1, 4)$, width = 3 units

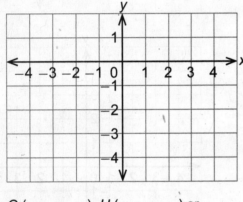 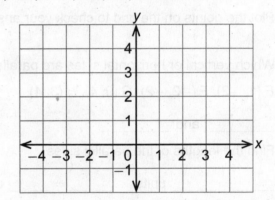

   $G(\quad, \quad), H(\quad, \quad)$ or $R(\quad, \quad), S(\quad, \quad)$ or

   $G(\quad, \quad), H(\quad, \quad)$ $R(\quad, \quad), S(\quad, \quad)$

3. The base of a parallelogram ABCD is parallel to an axis. Find the length of the base, and then predict the coordinates of point D. Plot the points to check your answer.

   a) $A(-5, -3), B(-4, -1), C(-1, -1)$ b) $A(-3, 0), B(-3, -2), C(3, -1)$

   length of base = ____ units, $D(\quad, \quad)$ length of base = ____ units, $D(\quad, \quad)$

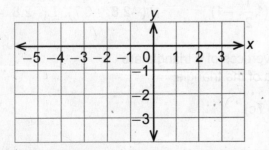 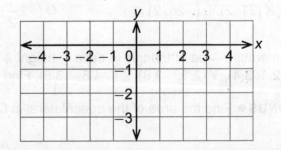

G6-26 Area on Coordinate Grids

1. a) Draw a line through points (3, 4) and (−1, 4). Label the line *m*.
Extend it across the grid.

b) Draw a line through points (−1, −1) and (−2, −1). Label the line *n*.
Extend it across the grid.

c) Which of the four points in a) and b) are on the same vertical line?

(,   ) and (,   )

Find the distance between these points using the coordinates.

_____ = _____

d) Draw another vertical line. Write the coordinates of the points
where the vertical line you drew meets lines *m* and *n*.

(,   ) and (,   )

What is the distance between these points? _____

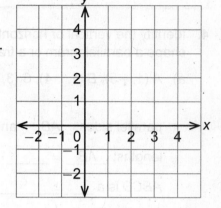

> The distance between parallel lines is the same no matter where you measure it.

2. a) Amy drew a line *u* through points (254, 67) and (−34.8, 67) and a line *v* through
points (−24.12, 2) and (143, 2).

What is the distance between the lines *u* and *v*? _____

b) Steve drew a line *w* through points (25.4, 6.7) and (25.4, −8) and a line *v* through
points (−24.1, 2.1) and (−24.1, −2.79).

What is the distance between the lines *w* and *v*? _____

> **REMINDER ▶** The height of a parallelogram or a trapezoid is the distance between the bases.

3. Which horizontal or vertical lines are parallel? Calculate the height of the shape, and
then plot the points to check your answer.

a) *A* (1, −2), *B* (−1, 3), *C* (3, 3), *D* (5, −2)

parallel sides: _____ and _____

height: _____

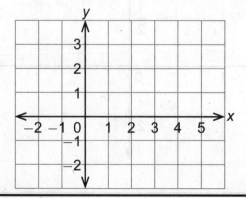

b) *E* (−2, −2), *F* (−2, 2), *G* (3, 3), *H* (3, 0)

parallel sides: _____ and _____

height: _____

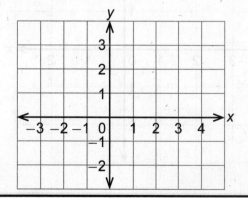

4. Identify the vertical or horizontal sides that are parallel and find their lengths. Is the shape a parallelogram or a trapezoid? What is the height of the shape?

a) *A* (1, −5), *B* (1, −4), *C* (3, 13), *D* (3, 12)

parallel sides: __*AB*__ and __*CD*__

lengths: __*AB*__ = _____ __*CD*__ = _____

ABCD is a _____

height: _____

b) *E* (−100, 235), *F* (−100, −12), *G* (387, −12), *H* (387, 143)

parallel sides: _____ and _____

lengths: _____ = _____ _____ = _____

EFGH is a _____

height: _____

c) *I* (−1.23, 2.4), *J* (−1.23, −3.21), *K* (5.6, −3.21), *L* (1.23, 2.4)

parallel sides: _____ and _____

lengths: _____ = _____ _____ = _____

IJKL is a _____

height: _____

d) *M* $(1\frac{1}{3}, 1\frac{2}{3})$, *N* $(5\frac{1}{6}, -1\frac{5}{6})$, *O* $(0, -1\frac{5}{6})$, *P* $(-3\frac{5}{6}, 1\frac{2}{3})$

parallel sides: _____ and _____

lengths: _____ = _____ _____ = _____

MNOP is a _____

height: _____

Area of a parallelogram = base × height or $A = b \times h$

Area of a trapezoid = (base 1 + base 2) × height ÷ 2 or $A = (b_1 + b_2) \times h \div 2$

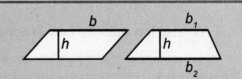

---

5. Plot the vertices of the quadrilateral. Find the length of the bases and the height of the shape. Then find the area of the quadrilateral. Include the units in your answer.

a) (1.6, 1.8), (1.6, −0.7), (−2.8, −0.3), (−2.8, −2.8)

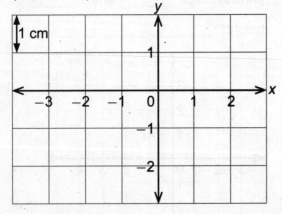

b) $(-1, \frac{1}{2})$, $(-1\frac{1}{4}, -\frac{3}{4})$, $(1\frac{1}{4}, -\frac{3}{4})$, $(\frac{3}{4}, \frac{1}{2})$

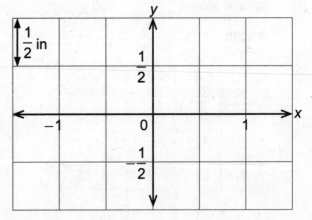

G6-27 Reflections

When a point is **reflected** in a mirror line, the point and the resulting point (called the **image**) are the same distance from the mirror line.

The line between the point and its image is **perpendicular** to the mirror line.

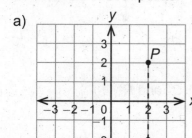

1. Reflect point P using the x-axis as a mirror line. Label the image point P'. Write the coordinates of both points.

a)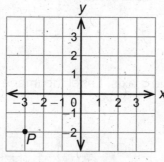

P (2 , 2) → P' (2 , −2)

b)

P (,   ) → P' (,   )

c)

P (,   ) → P' (,   )

2. Reflect points P, Q, and R through the x-axis. Label the image points P', Q', and R', and write their coordinates.

a)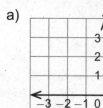

b)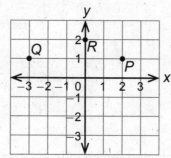

c)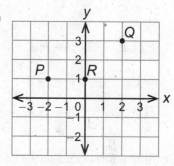

P (,   ) → P' (,   ) P (,   ) → P' (,   ) P (,   ) → P' (,   )

Q (,   ) → Q' (,   ) Q (,   ) → Q' (,   ) Q (,   ) → Q' (,   )

R (,   ) → R' (,   ) R (,   ) → R' (,   ) R (,   ) → R' (,   )

3. Compare the coordinates of the points and the images in Question 2.
   Which coordinate changes when a point is reflected through the x-axis? _____

   What happens to the other coordinate? _____

4. Predict the coordinates of the point when reflected through the x-axis.
   Use the grid to check your prediction. Hint: The opposite of 0 is 0.

   A (−2, 1) → A' (,   ) B (−3, −2) → B' (,   )

   C (0, −1) → C' (,   ) D (2, 3) → D' (,   )

   E (3, 0) → E' (,   )

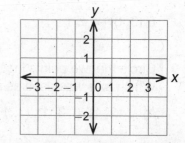

5. Reflect point *P* using the *y*-axis as a mirror line. Label the image point *P'*. Write the coordinates of both points.

a)

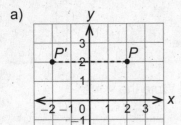

$P\,(\ 2\ ,\ 2\ ) \rightarrow P'\,(\ -2\ ,\ 2\ )$

b)

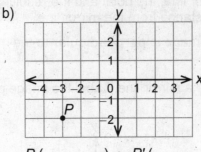

$P\,(\quad ,\quad) \rightarrow P'\,(\quad ,\quad)$

c)

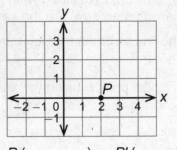

$P\,(\quad ,\quad) \rightarrow P'\,(\quad ,\quad)$

6. Reflect points *P*, *Q*, and *R* through the *y*-axis. Label the image points *P'*, *Q'*, and *R'*, and write their coordinates.

a)

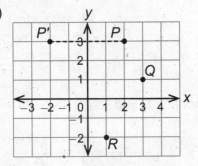

$P\,(\ 2\ ,\ 3\ ) \rightarrow P'\,(\ -2\ ,\ 3\ )$

$Q\,(\quad ,\quad) \rightarrow Q'\,(\quad ,\quad)$

$R\,(\quad ,\quad) \rightarrow R'\,(\quad ,\quad)$

b)

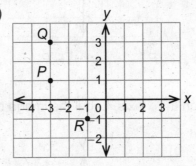

$P\,(\quad ,\quad) \rightarrow P'\,(\quad ,\quad)$

$Q\,(\quad ,\quad) \rightarrow Q'\,(\quad ,\quad)$

$R\,(\quad ,\quad) \rightarrow R'\,(\quad ,\quad)$

c)

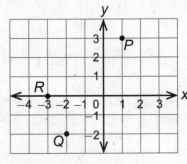

$P\,(\quad ,\quad) \rightarrow P'\,(\quad ,\quad)$

$Q\,(\quad ,\quad) \rightarrow Q'\,(\quad ,\quad)$

$R\,(\quad ,\quad) \rightarrow R'\,(\quad ,\quad)$

7. Compare the coordinates of the points and the images in Question 6.

Which coordinate changes when a point is reflected throught the *y*-axis? _____

What happens to the other coordinate? _____

8. Predict the coordinates of the points when reflected through the *y*-axis. Use the grid to check your prediction.

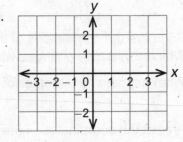

$A\,(-2,\,1) \rightarrow A'\,(\quad ,\quad)$ $B\,(-3,\,-2) \rightarrow B'\,(\quad ,\quad)$

$C\,(0,\,-1) \rightarrow C'\,(\quad ,\quad)$ $D\,(2,\,3) \rightarrow D'\,(\quad ,\quad)$

$E\,(3,\,0) \rightarrow E'\,(\quad ,\quad)$

9. Circle the two points that are reflections of each other through an axis. Which axis was used as a mirror line? How do you know?

a) $(-2,\,1),\ (-3,\,1),\ (3,\,1)$ b) $(-2,\,2),\ (-3,\,-2),\ (-2,\,-2)$

G6-28 Reflections (Advanced)

1. a) Reflect points P, Q, R, and S through the y-axis and then through the x-axis. Label the resulting image points P', Q', R', and S', and write the coordinates.

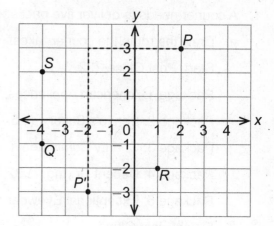

$P(\ 2\ ,\ 3\ ) \longrightarrow P'(\ -2\ ,\ -3\ )$

$Q(\quad,\quad) \longrightarrow Q'(\quad,\quad)$

$R(\quad,\quad) \longrightarrow R'(\quad,\quad)$

$S(\quad,\quad) \longrightarrow S'(\quad,\quad)$

b) Compare the coordinates of the points and their images in part a). How do the coordinates change when a point is reflected through the y-axis and then through the x-axis?

_____

_____

c) Reflect points W, X, Y, and Z through the x-axis. Then reflect the images through the y-axis. Label the resulting points W', X', Y' and Z', and write their coordinates.

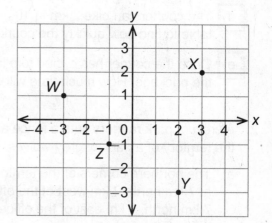

$W(\quad,\quad) \longrightarrow W'(\quad,\quad)$

$X(\quad,\quad) \longrightarrow X'(\quad,\quad)$

$Y(\quad,\quad) \longrightarrow Y'(\quad,\quad)$

$Z(\quad,\quad) \longrightarrow Z'(\quad,\quad)$

d) Compare the coordinates of the points and the images in part a). How do the coordinates change when a point is reflected through the x-axis and then through the y-axis?

_____

_____

e) Sam reflects a point (x, y) through the x-axis and then through the y-axis. Maxine reflects the same point through the y-axis first and then through the x-axis. Should they get the same result? Explain.

2. Predict the coordinates of each point when reflected through one axis and then through the other axis. Then check your prediction on a coordinate grid.

A (−2, 1)	B (−3, −2)	C (2.5, −1)	D (2, 3)	E (3, 0)	$F(0, -1\frac{1}{2})$	G (0,0)

G6-29 Applications of Coordinate Grids

1. A courier needs to deliver five packages.

   a) Draw the route the courier takes.

      Start: Post Office, (22, 37)

      Package 1: American Appliances, (22, −44)

      Package 2: Benito's Bakery, (−5, −44)

      Package 3: Charity Committee, (−5, −24)

      Package 4: Decent Driving, (−32, −24)

      Package 5: Exceptional Eyewear, (−32, 37)

      Finish: Post Office

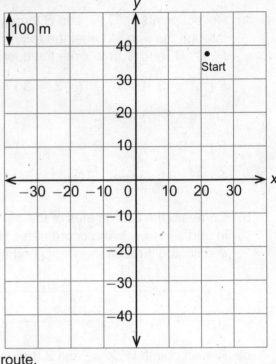

   b) What is the distance between Benito's Bakery and Charity Committee in squares? In meters?

   c) What is the total length of the route in meters?

   d) The courier can bike 2 km in 10 minutes. Use a ratio table to find how quickly the courier can cycle the whole route.

   e) Once the courier has cycled to a location, it takes the courier 3 minutes to drop off the package. How much time will delivering the packages take, including cycling?

2. A crew of park rangers puts a fence around the territory of a pack of grey wolves.

   a) The northern corners of the territory are at 7 km north, 2 km west of the office and 7 km north, 1 km east of the office. Mark the location of both corners on the grid.

   b) The territory is a rectangle with area 11.7 km². The boundaries run from north to south and from east to west. How long is the territory from north to south?

   c) Sketch the territory on the grid.

   d) What are the coordinates of the southern corners of the territory? (,   ) and (,   )

   e) How much fencing is needed to surround the territory?

   f) What is the approximate area of the lakes within the territory?

   g) What is the approximate area of the territory without the lakes?

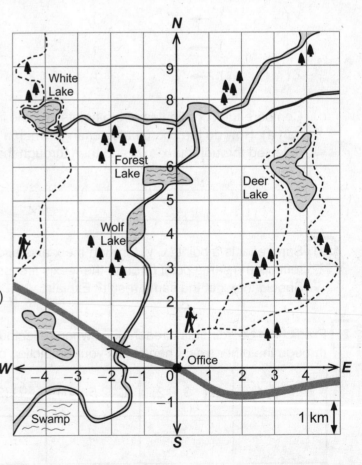

3. This is a map of Feral Cat Island.
   Round Lake is at point $(-1.5, 0)$.

Feral Cat Island

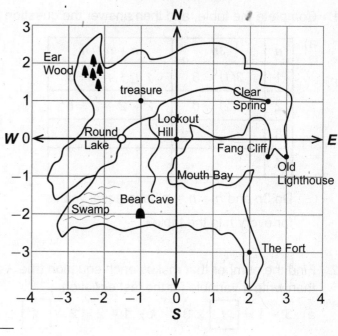

a) What is at point …

   i) $(-1, -2)$? _____

   ii) $(-1, 1)$? _____

   iii) $(2.5, 1)$? _____

   iv) $(2.5, -0.5)$? _____

b) What are the coordinates of …

   i) The Fort? _____

   ii) Lookout Hill? _____

   iii) Old Lighthouse? _____

c) Each square on the map represents
   1 square kilometer. What is …

   i) 1 km west of Bear Cave? _____

   ii) 3 km north of Bear Cave? _____

   iii) 1.5 km south of Clear Spring? _____

d) i) How far is the treasure from Clear Spring? _____

   ii) How far is Old Lighthouse from Fang Cliff? _____

BONUS ▶ A bear came out of Bear Cave and went 3.5 km north, then 1.5 km west,

and then 0.5 km north. Where did the bear end up? _____

4. A spacecraft measured some temperatures on Mars.

Time	2:00 a.m.	6:00 a.m.	10:00 a.m.
Temperature	−70°F	−10°F	50°F

a) Plot the data on the grid and join the points with a line.

b) Assume the temperature changes at the same rate during
   the morning. How much does the temperature rise …

   i) in 8 hours? ____   ii) in 1 hour? ____   iii) in 2 hours? ____

c) Fill in the table using your answers in part b). Plot the points
   on the graph and check your answer.

Time	3:00 a.m.	8:00 a.m.
Temperature		

d) At what time did the temperature reach 0°F? How do you know?

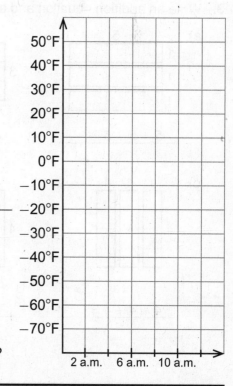

EE6-16 Equivalent Expressions

1. Complete the table, and then answer the question.

a)

n	3n	n + n + n
1	3(1) = 3	1 + 1 + 1 = 3
2	3(2) = 6	2 + 2 + 2 = 6
3		
4		

Do 3n and n + n + n have equal values

for every n in the table? _____

b)

n	2n + 2	2 × (n + 1)
1	2(1) + 2 = 4	2 × (1 + 1) = 4
2		
3		
4		

Do 2n + 2 and 2 × (n + 1) have equal values

for every n in the table? _____

2. Find the number that makes each equation true. Write the numbers in the boxes, and then write a variable for the last equation.

a) $3 \times 1 = \boxed{1} \times 3$

$3 \times 2 = \boxed{} \times 3$

$3 \times 3 = \boxed{} \times 3$

$3 \times 7 = \boxed{} \times 3$

$3 \times n = \boxed{} \times 3$

b) $1 + 2 = 2 + \boxed{1}$

$2 + 2 = 2 + \boxed{}$

$3 + 2 = 2 + \boxed{}$

$9 + 2 = 2 + \boxed{}$

$n + 2 = 2 + \boxed{}$

c) $1 + 1 + 1 = 3 \times \boxed{1}$

$2 + 2 + 2 = 3 \times \boxed{}$

$3 + 3 + 3 = 3 \times \boxed{}$

$8 + 8 + 8 = 3 \times \boxed{}$

$n + n + n = 3 \times \boxed{}$

d) $2 \times 1 - 1 = \boxed{1}$

$2 \times 2 - 2 = \boxed{}$

$2 \times 3 - 3 = \boxed{}$

$2 \times 4 - 4 = \boxed{}$

$2 \times n - n = \boxed{}$

3. Write an addition equation and a multiplication equation for the area of the figure.

a)

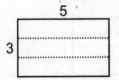

5 + 5 + 5 = _____

3 × 5 = _____

b)

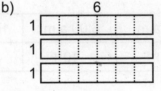

_____

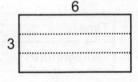

_____

c)

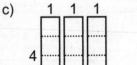

4 + 4 + 4 = _____

4 × 3 = _____

d)

_____

_____

Expressions and Equations 6-16

These two figures have equal areas: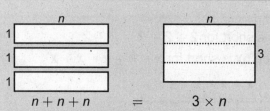

$$n + n + n \quad = \quad 3 \times n$$

The expressions $n + n + n$ and $3n$ are **equivalent expressions** because they have the same value for all n's.

4. Use the figures to write equivalent expressions.

a)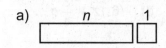

b)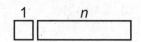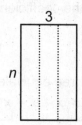

$$\underline{\quad n + 1 \quad} = \underline{\quad 1 + n \quad} \qquad \underline{\hspace{3cm}} = \underline{\hspace{3cm}}$$

c)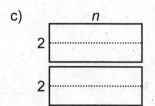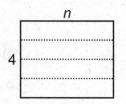

BONUS ▶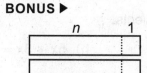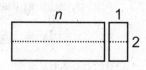

$$\underline{\hspace{3cm}} = \underline{\hspace{3cm}} \qquad \underline{\quad 2 \times (n + 1) \quad} = \underline{\hspace{3cm}}$$

Jeff puts two shapes together.

Jeff notices that $3 \times n + 3 \times 2 = 3 \times (n + 2)$. This shows the distributive property for algebraic expressions.

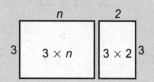 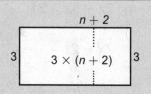

5. Use the distributive property to write an equivalent expression.

a) $4 \times (x - 3)$

$= 4 \times x - 4 \times 3$

$= 4x - 12$

So, $4 \times (x - 3)$ and $\underline{4x - 12}$ are equivalent.

b) $5 \times (n + 3)$

$=$

$=$

So, $5 \times (n + 3)$ and $\underline{\hspace{2cm}}$ are equivalent.

c) $(2 + t) \times 6$

BONUS ▶ $(5 - 3) \times x$

6. Use the distributive property to write an equivalent expression.

a) $3x + 6$

$= \underline{\ 3\ } \times (\underline{\quad} + \underline{\quad})$

b) $4x + 12$

$= \underline{\quad} \times (\underline{\quad} + \underline{\quad})$

c) $10y + 15$

$= \underline{\quad} \times (\underline{\quad} + \underline{\quad})$

EE6-17 Solving Algebraic Equations

> The expression 5×2 is short for $2 + 2 + 2 + 2 + 2$.
>
> Similarly, the expression $5x$ is short for $x + x + x + x + x$.
>
> $$\underbrace{x + x + x + x + x}_{5x} = \underbrace{x + x}_{} \; \underbrace{+ \; x + x + x}_{}$$
> $$5x \qquad = \quad 2x \; + \quad 3x$$
>
> $5x$ and $2x + 3x$ are equivalent expressions. In the expression $5x$, the number 5 is called the **coefficient**.

1. Circle the coefficients in each expression.

   a) ⑦w

   b) $0.5k - 11y$

   c) $2x - 5y$

   d) $-6.1z + \dfrac{3}{4}q$

2. Write three equivalent expressions for $6x$.

   $6x = \underbrace{x + x + x}_{} + \underbrace{x + x + x}_{}$

   $6x = \quad 3x \quad + \quad 3x$

   $6x = \underbrace{x + x}_{} + \underbrace{x + x + x + x}_{}$

   $6x = \qquad +$

   $6x = \underbrace{x}_{} + \underbrace{x + x + x + x + x}_{}$

   $6x = \quad +$

3. Add by adding the coefficients.

   a) $3x + 5x = \underline{\;\;8x\;\;}$

   b) $5x + 3x = \underline{\qquad}$

   c) $7x + x = \underline{\qquad}$

   d) $5x + 6x = \underline{\qquad}$

   e) $19x + x = \underline{\qquad}$

   BONUS ▶ $2x + 5x + 4x = \underline{\qquad}$

4. Group the x's together, and then solve the equation for x.

   a) $2x + 5x = 21$

   b) $3x + 2x = 15$

   c) $6x + x = 28$

   $7x = 21$

   $x = \dfrac{21}{7} = 3$

   d) $4x + 5x = 18$

   e) $8x + 3x = 22$

   BONUS ▶ $5x + 2x = 0$

5. Fill in the blank.

   a) $3 - 3 = \underline{\qquad}$

   b) $8 - 8 = \underline{\qquad}$

   c) $132 - 132 = \underline{\qquad}$

   d) $3.1 - 3.1 = \underline{\qquad}$

   e) $\dfrac{1}{2} - \dfrac{1}{2} = \underline{\qquad}$

   f) $2\dfrac{1}{3} - 2\dfrac{1}{3} = \underline{\qquad}$

   g) $1.53 - 1.53 = \underline{\qquad}$

   h) $\dfrac{4}{3} - \dfrac{4}{3} = \underline{\qquad}$

   i) $x - x = \underline{\qquad}$

   j) $\dfrac{3}{5} + 3 - 3 = \underline{\qquad}$

   k) $5\dfrac{1}{4} + 3 - 3 = \underline{\qquad}$

   l) $x + 3 - 3 = \underline{\qquad}$

Every time you see a number or variable subtracted from itself in an equation (For example: $3 - 3$, $5 - 5$, $8 - 8$, $x - x$), you can cross out both numbers or variables because they will add to 0. Crossing out parts of an equation that make 0 is called **cancelling**.

6. Fill in the blank by crossing out numbers or variables that add to 0.

a) $4 + \cancel{8} - \cancel{8} = \underline{\ 4\ }$

b) $5 + 2 - 2 = \underline{\hspace{1cm}}$

c) $7 + 1 - 1 = \underline{\hspace{1cm}}$

d) $8 + 6.2 - 6.2 = \underline{\hspace{1cm}}$

e) $\dfrac{1}{2} + 7 - \dfrac{1}{2} = \underline{\hspace{1cm}}$

f) $\dfrac{7}{3} + 9 - \dfrac{7}{3} = \underline{\hspace{1cm}}$

g) $4 + 3 - 3 + 7 - 7 = \underline{\hspace{1cm}}$

h) $0.5 + 2 - 2 + 4 - 0.5 = \underline{\hspace{1cm}}$

i) $7 + x - 7 = \underline{\hspace{1cm}}$

j) $x + 129 - 129 = \underline{\hspace{1cm}}$

k) $x + 4.6 - 4.6 = \underline{\hspace{1cm}}$

l) $x + n - n = \underline{\hspace{1cm}}$

7. Rewrite the expression as a sum of individual variables and then cancel. Write what's left.

a) $5x - 2x = \underline{\ 3x\ }$

b) $4x - x = \underline{\hspace{1cm}}$

c) $5x - x + 2x = \underline{\hspace{1cm}}$

$x + x + x + \cancel{x} + \cancel{x} - \cancel{x} - \cancel{x}$

8. Subtract by subtracting the coefficients.

a) $7x - 5x = \underline{\hspace{1cm}}$

b) $8x - 4x = \underline{\hspace{1cm}}$

c) $4x - 2x + 3x = \underline{\hspace{1cm}}$

d) $9x - 3x + 4x = \underline{\hspace{1cm}}$

e) $7x - 5x + x = \underline{\hspace{1cm}}$

f) $5x - 5x + 2x = \underline{\hspace{1cm}}$

9. Group the x's together, and then solve for x.

a) $8x - 3x + x = 30$

b) $5x + x - x - 2x = 0.21$

c) $7x - 3x - 2x = 2.2$

d) $1.4 = 4x - x + x + 3x$

e) $9x - 2x - 2x = 2$

f) $3.2 = 4x + 3x - 3x - 4x + 4x$

10. Solve for x. Check your answer.

a) $x + 0.3 = 1.5$

$x + 0.3 - 0.3 = 1.5 - 0.3$

$x = 1.2$

Check by replacing x with your answer: $1.2 + 0.3 = \mathbf{1.5}\ \checkmark$

b) $x - 0.4 = 2$

$x - 0.4 + 0.4 = 2 + 0.4$

c) $1.5 + x = 1.9$

d) $3.1 = x + 1.4$

e) $0.9 = x - 4.6$

f) $2x = 4.6$

g) $0.8x = 5.6$

h) $1.5x = 15$

i) $1.1x = 4.4$

EE6-18 Word Problems

To solve word problems, you turn the words into algebraic expressions. The words give clues to the operations you need to use. Here are some of the clues for different operations:

Add	Subtract	Multiply	Divide
increased by	less than	product	divided by
sum	difference	times	divided into
more than	decreased by	twice as many	
	reduced by		

1. Match each algebraic expression with the correct description.

2 more than a number	$4x$	2 divided into a number	$3x$
a number divided by 3	$x - 2$	a number reduced by 4	$x \div 2$
2 less than a number	$x + 2$	a number times 3	$x + 3$
the product of a number and 4	$x - 3$	twice as many as a number	$x - 4$
a number decreased by 3	$x \div 3$	a number increased by 3	$2x$

2. Write an algebraic expression for the description.

a) four more than a number

b) a number decreased by 8.5

c) a number divided by 8

d) two less than a number

e) a number increased by 2.9

f) a number reduced by 4

g) five times a number

h) 6 divided into a number

i) the product of 7 and a number

j) twice as many as a number

k) the sum of a number and 4.7

l) the product of a number and 3.3

When solving word problems, the word "is" translates to the equal sign, "=".

Example: "Two more than a number is seven" can be written as $x + 2 = 7$.

---

3. Solve the problem by first writing an equation.

a) Four more than a number is eighteen.

b) Five less than a number is 12.4.

c) Five times a number is thirty.

d) Six times a number is forty-two.

e) Six divided into a number is 1.5.

f) The product of a number and 5 is two.

g) A number multiplied by two is thirty-six.

h) A number multiplied by three is eighteen.

i) Three divided into a number is 2.3.

j) Twice a number is 10.6.

k) Three times a number is 3.6.

BONUS ▶ Half of a number is 1 more than 4.

4. a) Write an expression for the perimeter of the shape (x stands for the length of the unknown sides). Then write an equivalent expression for the perimeter.

i)

ii)

iii)

$\underline{\quad x + x + x = 3x \quad}$ 　　　 $\underline{\hspace{5cm}}$ 　　　 $\underline{\hspace{5cm}}$

b) The perimeter of each shape in part a) is 12. Find the unknown side lengths.

5. Write an equation to find the length of the missing side.

a)

b)

c)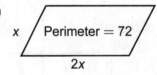

$\underline{\hspace{4cm}}$ 　　 $\underline{\hspace{4cm}}$ 　　 $\underline{\hspace{4cm}}$

6. Mark's dad is three times older than Mark. The difference between their ages is 24 years. How old is Mark?

7. The height of the water in a water tank is 42 inches. The height of the water in the tank decreases 6 inches each day. After how many days will the water tank be empty?

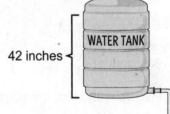

8. The sum of two numbers is 45. One number is twice the other number. Write an equation and find the numbers.

9. Chandra is five times as old as Rita. The sum of their ages is 42. How old are Chandra and Rita?

BONUS ▶ Binh paid $51 for two pairs of pants. He bought the first pair at the regular price, but the second pair at half price. What is the regular price for one pair of pants? Hint: Let x be the price of the second pair.

Expressions and Equations 6-18 　　　　　　　　　　　　　　　　　　　 **115**

EE6-19 Graphs and Equations

1. For each set of points, write a list of ordered pairs and complete the table. Then write an equation that tells you the relationship between *x* and *y*.

a)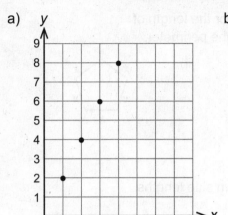

b)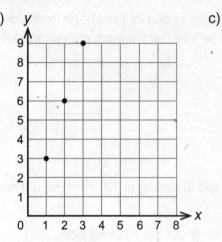

c)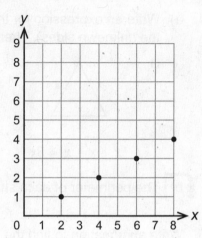

Ordered Pairs	x	y
(1 , 2)	1	2
(,)		
(,)		
(,)		

$2 \times x = y$

$or \; y = 2x$

Ordered Pairs	x	y
(,)		
(,)		
(,)		
(,)		

Ordered Pairs	x	y
(,)		
(,)		
(,)		
(,)		

2. Complete the table and plot the points on the grid for the given rule.

a) Multiply by 2 and add 1

x	2x + 1 = y
1	2 × 1 + 1 = 3
2	2 × 2 + 1 = 5
3	
4	

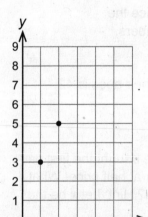

b) Multiply by 3 and subtract 3

x	3x − 3 = y
1	
2	
3	
4	

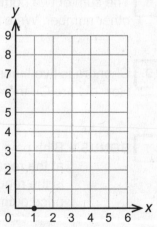

3. 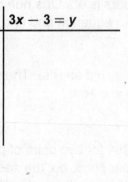 Draw a coordinate grid (like those above) on grid paper and plot the following ordered pairs: (1, 3), (3, 5), (5, 7), and (7, 9).

4. Make a table for each set of points on the coordinate grid. Write a rule for each table
    that tells you how to calculate *y* from *x*.

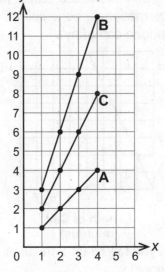

Graph A			Graph B			Graph C	
x	*y*		*x*	*y*		*x*	*y*

    Rule: $y =$ ___ $y =$ ___ $y =$ ___

5. Write a list of ordered pairs based on the table provided. Plot the ordered pairs on
    the graph and connect the points to form a line.

a)

x	*y*		
0	1	(,)	
1	2	(,)	
2	3	(,)	
3	4	(,)	

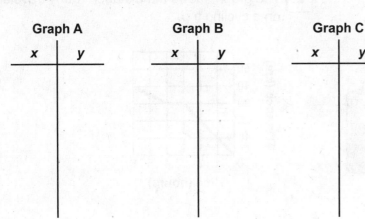

b)

x	*y*		
0	0	(,)	
1	2	(,)	
2	4	(,)	
3	6	(,)	

c)

x	*y*		
0	0	(,)	
2	1	(,)	
4	2	(,)	
6	3	(,)	

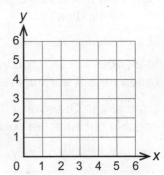

d)

x	*y*		
1	0	(,)	
2	1	(,)	
3	2	(,)	
4	3	(,)	

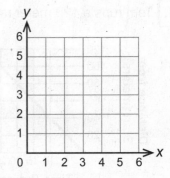

BONUS ▶ Write an equation that tells you the relationship between *x* and *y* for each
table in Question 5.

a) $y = x +$ ☐   b) $y =$ ☐ x c) $y =$ d) $y =$

EE6-20 Dependent and Independent Variables

1. The graph shows the cost of making an international phone call with a cell phone company.

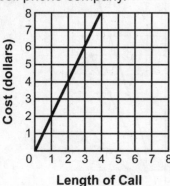

Length of Call (minutes)

a) If you talked for 2 minutes, how much would you pay?

b) What is the cost for a 1 minute call?

c) How much would you pay to talk for 10 minutes?

2. The graph shows the distance Kathy traveled on a cycling trip.

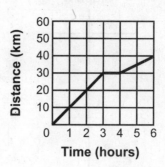

Time (hours)

a) How far had Kathy cycled after 2 hours?

b) How far had Kathy traveled after 6 hours?

c) Did Kathy rest at all on her trip? How do you know?

In an equation with two variables, the **dependent variable** represents the output or effect and the **independent variable** represents the input or cause.

Example: In Question 1, the length of the call is the independent variable and the cost is the dependent variable because the cost depends on the length of call.

Mathematicians usually use the *x*-axis for independent variables and the *y*-axis for dependent variables.

---

3. Tom runs a 120 meter race.

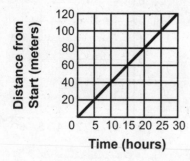

Time (hours)

a) What are the dependent and independent variables?

b) How far from the start was Tom after

   i) 10 seconds?   ii) 25 seconds?

c) If he continues running at the same rate, how far will Tom be after 1 minute?

4. The graph shows the cost of renting a bike from Mika's store.

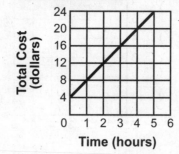

Time (hours)

a) What are the dependent and independent variables?

b) How much would you pay to rent the bike for

   i) 2 hours?   ii) 4 hours?   iii) 3 hours?

c) How much do you pay for the bike before you have even ridden it?

5. For each table below, write a rule that tells
- how the input changes,
- how the output changes, and
- the relation between the input and output.

Example:

Input	Output
1	3
2	6
3	9
4	12

- The numbers in the input column increase by 1 each time.
- The numbers in the output column increase by 3 each time.
- Multiply the input by 3 to get the output.

a)

Input	Output
1	3
2	12
3	18

b)

Input	Output
1	9
2	18
3	27

c)

Input	Output
1	11
2	22
3	33

d)

Input	Output
1	7
2	14
3	21

e)

Input	2.5	3.0	4.0	5.5	7.5	10.0	13.0
Output	5	6	8	11	15	20	26

f)

Input	1	2	3	4	5	6	7
Output	1	4	9	16	25	36	49

g)

Input	1	2	3	4	5	6	7
Output	2.1	4.2	6.3	8.4	10.5	12.6	14.7

6. The table shows the number of kilometers Janelle can run in 15 minutes. Complete the table. Note: Assume she keeps running at the same rate.

Distance	Time (seconds)	Time (minutes)	Time (hours)
2.3 km		15	$\frac{1}{4}$
4.6 km			
	2,700		

EE6-21 Introduction to Inequalities

Tan weighs 80 pounds, and Walter weighs more than 80 pounds. If *w* is Walter's weight, then the **inequality** $80 < w$ represents what we know about Walter's weight.

Walter's weight could be 90 pounds (90 is more than 80), so 90 is one **solution** for the inequality $80 < w$.

We can use a number line to show the inequality.

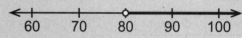

- The thick black part of the number line shows all the possible solutions.

- There is a white circle at 80 because Walter's weight cannot be 80 ($80 < 80$ is not correct).

1. Write an inequality for the phrase.

   a) *w* is less than 7.   <u>$w < 7$</u>

   b) *w* is greater than 50.   _____

   c) *w* is less than 0.   _____

   d) *w* is greater than −5.   _____

   e) *w* is less than −7.   _____

   f) *w* is greater than 0.   _____

2. Write the meaning of the inequality.

   a) $w < 5$ <u>*w is less than 5.*</u>

   b) $w > -4$ _____

   c) $w > 0$ _____

   d) $w < -5$ _____

Every inequality can be written in two ways. For example, the inequality "*w* is greater than 80" can be written as "80 is less than *w*."

3. Write the inequality in another way.

   a) *w* is less than 20.   <u>*20 is greater than w.*</u>

   b) *w* is greater than 4.   _____

   c) *w* is greater than 0.   _____

   d) *w* is greater than −5.   _____

4. Circle the numbers that are solutions for the inequality $80 < b$.

   75   91   81   69   93.5   79.9   80.5   100   80

5. Connect each inequality on top to its solutions on the bottom.
   Note: Each inequality has more than one solution.

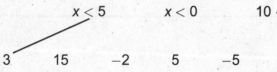

$x < 5$ $x < 0$ $10 < x$

3   15   −2   5   −5   23   10

6. Write an inequality for the number line.

a)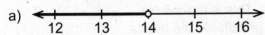

    <u> x < 14 </u>

b)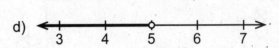

    <u>   </u>

c)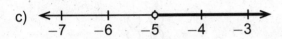

    <u>   </u>

d)

    <u>   </u>

7. Write an inequality for the story. Let x represent the unknown. If the solution is always a positive number, write "and $x > 0$."

a) Susan is 12 years old. Susan's sister is younger than Susan.

    <u> $x < 12$ and $x > 0$ </u>

b) Julius has $7.50 and Michael has less money than Julius.

    <u>   </u>

c) The temperature will be less than 12 degrees on Sunday.

    <u>   </u>

d) Tyrone is younger than his 17-year-old brother.

    <u>   </u>

8. Draw a thick line to show the solution of the inequality on the given number line. Part a) is done for you.

a) $x < 9$

b) $x > 17$

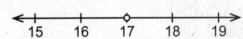

c) $x > 0$

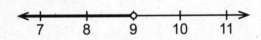

d) $x < -4$

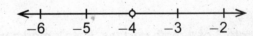

BONUS ▶ Malina is going shopping. She plans to buy a shirt for $7, a pair of pants for $15, and a pair of shoes that is more expensive than the pair of pants. Write an inequality to represent the amount of money that she needs to pay for the items. Show the inequality on a number line.

SP6-1 Mean

1. Move beads until all stacks have the same number of beads. This is the **mean** number of beads in a stack. Cross out the beads you move and shade the beads you draw in new positions to find the mean. The first one is done for you.

a) 4 2

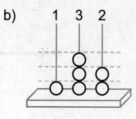

Mean: _3_

b) 1 3 2

Mean: ____

c) 3 3 0

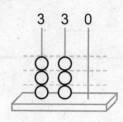

Mean: ____

d) 4 2 1 5

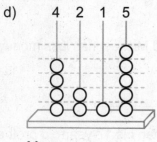

Mean: ____

e) 2 3 6 5 4

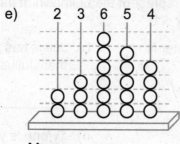

Mean: ____

f) 1 5 0 0 4

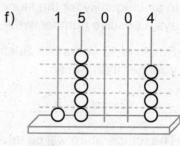

Mean: ____

2. Draw stacks of beads with the number of beads shown. Move beads to find the mean. The first one is started for you.

a) 1 6 4 1

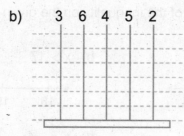

Mean: ____

b) 3 6 4 5 2

Mean: ____

c) 6 6 0 3 4 5

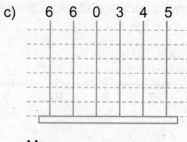

Mean: ____

3. Kate wrote 3 of 4 math quizzes. Kate's marks were 3 out of 6, 4 out of 6, and 5 out of 6.

a) Move beads to find Kate's mean quiz mark in the following 2 cases:

i) Her teacher does not count the quiz she didn't write.

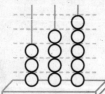

Beads: _12_

Stacks: _3_

Mean: ____

ii) Her teacher counts the quiz she didn't write as 0 out of 6.

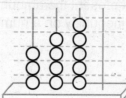

Beads: ____

Stacks: ____

Mean: ____

b) Do you think Kate would want her teacher to count all 4 quizzes? Explain.

4. a) Write the total number of beads and stacks. Move beads to find the mean.

i)

Beads: __15__

Stacks: _____

Mean: _____

ii)

Beads: _____

Stacks: _____

Mean: _____

iii)

Beads: _____

Stacks: _____

Mean: _____

b) Use the three numbers from each picture in part a) to write a division equation.

i) ___15 ÷ 5 = 3___   ii) _____   iii) _____

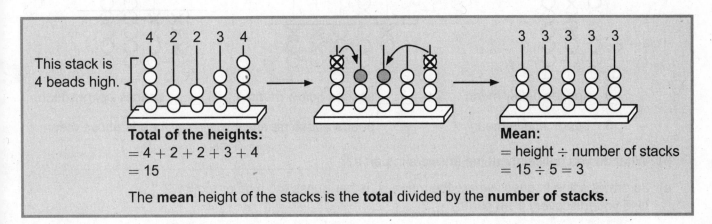

This stack is
4 beads high.

Total of the heights:
= 4 + 2 + 2 + 3 + 4
= 15

Mean:
= height ÷ number of stacks
= 15 ÷ 5 = 3

The **mean** height of the stacks is the **total** divided by the **number of stacks**.

5. Calculate the mean using division.

	Data Set	Total	Number of Stacks	Mean
a)	7 3	7 + 3 = 10	2	10 ÷ 2 = 5
b)	12 0 4 8 6			
c)	1 16 8 11 9			
d)	21 6 12 1			
	BONUS ▶			
e)	100 400 300 200			
f)	1,000 1,400 600			

6. Find the mean using division and draw a horizontal line to show it.

a)

$$15 \div 3 = 5$$

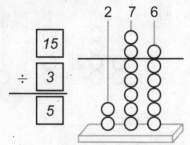

b)

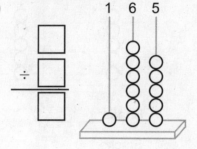

c)

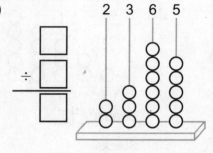

7. a) The line shows the mean. Count the spaces below it and the beads above it.

i)

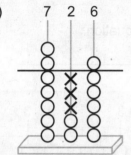

___3___ spaces *below* mean

___3___ beads *above* mean

ii)

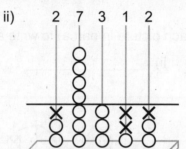

_____ spaces *below* mean

_____ beads *above* mean

iii)

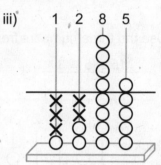

_____ spaces *below* mean

_____ beads *above* mean

b) What do you notice about the answers in part a)? _____

c) Jo draws a line to guess where the mean is. Is her guess too high or too low?
Use your discovery from part b).

i)

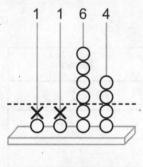

too _____

ii)

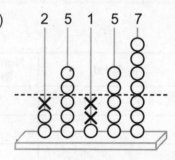

too _____

iii)

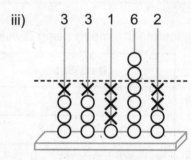

too _____

8. a) Create a new data set by adding 4 to each data value.

	Data Set						Mean	New Data Set (Each Data Value + 4)			New Mean
i)	9	9	6				8	13	13	10	12
ii)	2	6	9	3							
iii)	0	1	1	4	5	1					

b) Complete the formula for finding the new mean: new mean = old mean + _____ .

9. a) Find the mean weight of the newborn animals. Compare the weight in **bold** to the mean.

Animal	Weight in Pounds	Mean Weight	Greater Than, Less Than, Equal To
Elephant Calf	260, 300, **200**, 240	250	**200** is ___*less than*___ the mean
Beluga Calf	**185**, 200, 170, 165		**185** is _____ the mean
Seal Pup	35, 20, **25**, 20		**25** is _____ the mean

b) In zoos, a newborn animal that weighs less than the mean weight for its kind may need extra care. Which animal from part a) may need extra care: the 200 pound elephant, the 185 pound beluga, or the 25 pound seal?

_____

10. On average people drink about a liter of water a day, which is 100 liters in 100 days. The mean cost of 100 liters of tap water is 5¢. The mean cost of 100 liters of bottled water is $100.

a) Complete the table.

	Cost of Water for:	Tap Water 5¢/100 Liters	Bottled Water $100/100 Liters
i)	a family of 2 for 100 days	5¢ × 2 = 10¢	$100 × 2 = $200
ii)	a family of 3 for 100 days		
iii)	a family of 4 for 100 days		

b) How much more does it cost each family to drink bottled water than to drink tap water for 100 days?

i) a family of 2 ___$200 − 10¢ = $199.90___

ii) a family of 3 _____

iii) a family of 4 _____

11. a) Nathan's and Shyla's overall science marks are the mean of 4 quizzes. All quizzes were out of 10. Calculate the mean.

	Quiz 1	Quiz 2	Quiz 3	Quiz 4	Mean of All 4 Quizzes
Nathan's Quiz Marks	10	0	10	0	
Shyla's Quiz Marks	5	5	5	5	

b) What do you notice about the students' mean science marks?

c) Describe any patterns you see in each student's quiz marks.

d) If the only information you had were the means, would you have any way of knowing about the patterns you found? _____

SP6-2 Mean, Median, and Range

To find the **median** of a set of data, put the data in order from lowest to highest. Count from either end until you reach the center.

2   3   ⑥   7   11

The median is 6.

2   3   ⟨7   9⟩   11   15

The median is 8, halfway between 7 and 9.

1. Circle the middle number or numbers. Find the median of the set of data.

   a) 2   2   3   3   4   16   b) 1   2   4   6   7   c) 14   17   19   23

   Median: _____   Median: _____   Median: _____

2. Order the data from lowest to highest. Circle the middle number or numbers.
   Find the median.

   a) 6   4   8   2   7   b) 3   2   8   3   c) 1   4   9   7   26   13

   __ __ __ __ __   __ __ __ __   __ __ __ __ __ __

   Median: _____   Median: _____   Median: _____

3. a) Find the mean and median of the data.

   b) Describe how the mean changes as the
      last data value increases.

   c) Describe how the median changes as the
      last data value increases.

Data Set					Median	Mean
1	1	2	5	6	2	3
1	1	2	5	11	2	4
1	1	2	5	16		
1	1	2	5	21		

   d) Graph the data sets from part a). Draw an "**X**" on the median and circle the mean.

   1   1   2   5   6

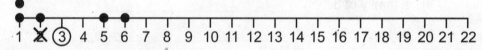

   1   1   2   5   11

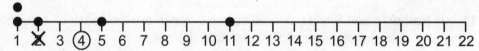

   1   1   2   5   16

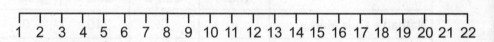

   1   1   2   5   21

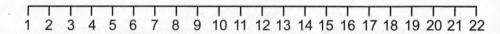

 BONUS ▶

   a) Find the mean and median of the data: 1   2   2   4   6   231

   b) Explain why it would be difficult to find the mean of this data set using beads.

The **range** of a data set shows how far apart the hightest and lowest values are from each other.

range = highest value − lowest value

Example: The range of the data set   7, 2, 6, 11, 3   is 9 because   11 − 2 = 9.

4. Find the highest value. Find the lowest value. Find the range.

a) 474, 447, 44, 444, 47, 477

highest: _____   lowest: _____

_____ − _____ = _____
highest   lowest   range

b) 623, 326, 236, 632, 263, 362

highest: _____   lowest: _____

_____ − _____ = _____
highest   lowest   range

5. Use the lowest value and the range to find the highest value.

a) 2, 4, 5, _____   range = 6

_____ − _____ = _____
highest   lowest   range

b) 16, 22, 24, 30, 34, 37, _____   range = 23

_____ − _____ = _____
highest   lowest   range

6. In which group would you expect to see a wider range of height measurements: in all the students at Springville Elementary School or in only the kindergarten students? Explain.

7. The set shows the temperature (°F) for 1 week. Find the range.

	Sun	Mon	Tue	Wed	Thu	Fri	Sat
a)	75	77	74	79	74	79	76
b)	55	56	71	62	79	71	76

a) Range: _____ − _____ = _____

b) Range: _____ − _____ = _____

8. a) Find the median and range of the data set.

Data Set					Median	Range
i)	8	11	14	15	17	*14*	*9*
ii)	3	6	9				
iii)	1	16	18	23			

b) Add 10 to the highest value in the sets from part a). Then find the new median and range.

Data Set					Median	Range
i)	8	11	14	15	<u>27</u>	*14*	*19*
ii)	3	6	___				
iii)	1	16	18	___			

c) Did the median change when you changed the highest value? _____

d) Did the range change when you changed the highest value? _____

BONUS ▶ Create two data sets with the given median and range. You can use the same value more than once in a set.

Set 1: ____ ____ ____ *12* ____ ____ ____   median: 12   range: 5

Set 2: ____ ____ ____ ____ ____ ____ ____   median: 12   range: 15

SP6-3 Frequency

The **frequency** of a value is the number of times it occurs in a data set.

Example: 1, 3, 0, 1, 1, 3, 1, 1, 1, 0, 1 ⟶

Data Value	Tally	Frequency
0	II	2
1	ℍℍ II	7
2		0
3	II	2

Record all values within the range even if they don't occur in the set.

1. a) Transfer the data into the tally chart. Cross out each number as you mark it in the chart.

 i) 0̸, 3̸, 2̸, 0̸, 2̸, 2̸, 3̸

Data Value	Tally	Frequency
0	II	2
1		
2	III	
3	II	

 ii) 4̸, 3̸, 1, 4, 3, 3, 1, 4, 4, 3, 4

Data Value	Tally	Frequency
1		
2		
3	I	
4	I	

 b) How many numbers are in the data set? i) __7__ ii) _____

 c) How many tallies are in the frequency column? i) __7__ ii) _____

 d) What is the total of all the frequencies in the frequency column? i) _____ ii) _____

 e) If your answers to parts b), c), and d) aren't the same, find your mistake.

2. Answer the questions for the data set 0, 4, 3, 4, 4, 3.

 a) Find the sum of the data values.

 __0__ + __4__ + _____ + _____ + _____ + _____ = _____

 b) Order the data values from least to greatest: _____, _____, _____, _____, _____, _____

 c) Write how many times each data value occurs. Then find the sum.

 (__1__ × 0) + (_____ × 3) + (_____ × 4) = __0__ + _____ + _____ = _____

 d) Did you get the same answer in parts a) and c)? If not, find your mistake.

 e) Find the mean. $\dfrac{}{\text{mean}} = \dfrac{}{\text{total from c)}} \div \dfrac{}{\text{number of values}}$

3. Use the two methods for totaling from Question 2 to find the mean.

 a) 1, 0, 4, 4, 2, 7, 5, 5, 1, 1   b) 7, 7, 3, 7, 3, 3, 7, 7, 3, 3

 BONUS ▶ Find the mean of this set: 80, 80, 80, 20, 80, 20, 80, 20, 20, 20.

SP6-4 Dot Plots

All **dot plots** have:

- a number line
- a group of data points that are represented with a symbol such as ● or ✗

Some dot plots have a title and a label.

The number line can start at any value, including 0.

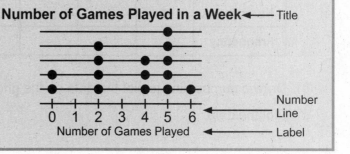

Number of Games Played in a Week ← Title

Number Line →

Number of Games Played ← Label

1. Use the dot plot to fill in the blanks.

   a) The most books read by any student was _____.

   b) How many students read exactly two books? _____

   c) The largest number of students read _____ books.

   d) The number of students in Sam's class is _____.

   e) _____ students read either one or two books.

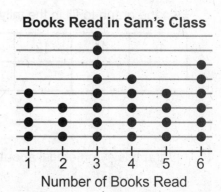

Books Read in Sam's Class

Number of Books Read

2. The survey data shows how many miles people walked in a week.

Miles Walked	1	2	3	4
Number of People	卌 III	卌 II		III

   a) Fill in the missing numbers on the number line.

   b) Plot the data.

   c) What answer was given most frequently? _____

   d) How many people walked at least two miles? _____

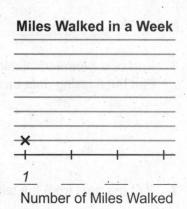

Miles Walked in a Week

Number of Miles Walked

3. Graphs A, B, and C have the same pattern of data: Which is not a dot plot? Explain.

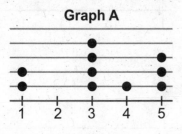

Graph A

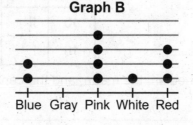

Graph B

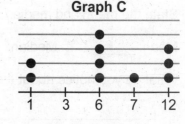

Graph C

4. a) Put the data into the tally chart. 3, 4, 5, 5, 4, 1, 5, 5, 3, 4, 5, 4

Number	1				5
Frequency					

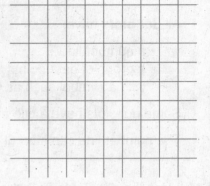

b) Draw a number line to plot the data on the grid provided.

c) Plot the data.

5. Use the graph to fill in the tally chart.

10	11	12	13	14	15

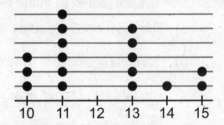

The graph is symmetrical about the center, 5.

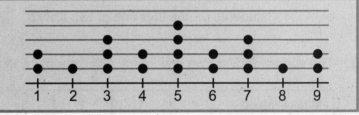

6. Part of a symmetrical data set, with center at 16, has been graphed. Plot the missing data on the dot plot. Use the fewest number of dots.

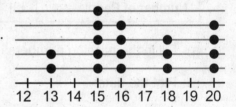

7. Plot the data from the tally chart on the graph.

a) Is the graph symmetrical? _____

b) The center of the graph is at _____ .

c) State the mean and median.

Mean: _____   Median: _____

12	I
13	II
14	IIII
15	II
16	I

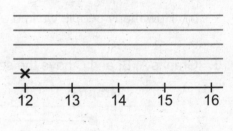

d) What do you notice about the median, the mean, and the center?

_____

_____

_____

_____

8. a) Use graphs A, B, C, and D to complete the table below.

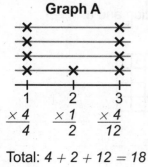

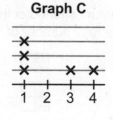

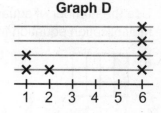

$$\frac{\times 4}{4} \quad \frac{\times 1}{2} \quad \frac{\times 4}{12}$$

Total: $4 + 2 + 12 = 18$

Mean: $18 \div 9 = 2$

Do your rough work like this in your notebook.

	Graph A	Graph B	Graph C	Graph D
Mean				
Median				
Is the graph symmetrical?				
Does the mean equal the median?				

b) What can you predict about the median and mean of symmetrical graphs?

9. Graphs A and B have the same shape, and graphs C and D have the same shape.

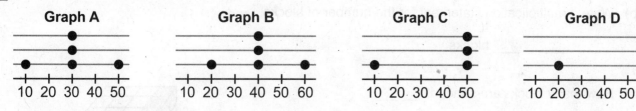

a) Will the mean and median of graph A be the same as those of graph B? Explain.

b) Will the mean and median of graph A be equal to each other? Explain.

c) Will the mean and median of graph C be the same as those of graph D? Explain.

10. Calculate the mean of graph A and then predict the means of graphs B, C, and D.

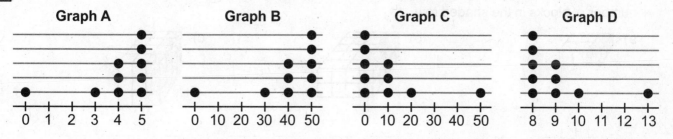

G6-30 Stacking Blocks

1. Use the number of squares in the shaded column to write an addition equation and a multiplication equation for the total number of squares.

   a)

   $\underline{3} + \underline{3} + \underline{3} + \underline{3}$

   $= \underline{12}$

   $\underline{4} \times \underline{3} = \underline{12}$

   b)

   ___ + ___

   = ___

   ___ × ___ = ___

   c)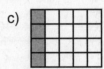

   ___ + ___ + ___ + ___ + ___

   = ___

   ___ × ___ = ___

2. How many blocks are in the shaded row?

   a)

   _____ blocks

   b)

   _____ blocks

   c)

   _____ blocks

3. a) Write an addition statement for the number of blocks. Use the number of blocks in the shaded row.

   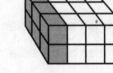

   ___ + ___ + ___ = ___ blocks

   b) Write a multiplication statement for the number of blocks.

   ___ × ___ = ___ blocks

4. a) How many blocks are shaded? _____

   b) Write an addition equation for the number of blocks in the shape.

   ___ + ___ + ___ + ___ = ___ blocks

   c) Write a multiplication equation for the same shape: ___ × 4 = ___ blocks

5. Write an addition and multiplication equation for the number of blocks. Use the number of blocks in the shaded row.

   a)

   ___ + ___ + ___

   = ___ blocks

   ___ × ___3___ = ___ blocks

   b)

   ___ + ___ + ___ + ___

   = ___ blocks

   ___ × ___ = ___ blocks

   c)

   ___ + ___ + ___

   = ___ blocks

   ___ × ___ = ___ blocks

6. Claire stacks blocks to make a tower. She finds the number of blocks in each tower by multiplying the number of blocks in the base by the number of layers.

a) Write a multiplication statement for the number of blocks in one layer.

___ × ___ = ___ blocks

b) Write a multiplication statement for the number of blocks in the tower. Use the number of blocks in the shaded layer.

i)

blocks in each layer   *number of layers*

___ × ___ × ___

= ___ blocks

ii)

___ × ___ × ___

= ___ blocks

iii)

___ × ___ × ___

= ___ blocks

7. Write a multiplication statement for the number of blocks

a)

___ × ___ × ___ = ___

b)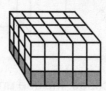

___ × ___ × ___ = ___

c)

___ × ___ × ___ = ___

8. How many blocks are on one side of the tower? What is the total number of blocks?

a) Number of blocks on one side = height × width

= __3__ × __2__ = __6__ blocks

Total number of blocks = height × width × length

= ___ × ___ × ___ = ___ blocks

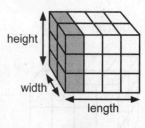

height

width

length

b) Number of blocks on one side = height × width

= ___ × ___ = ___ blocks

Total number of blocks = height × width × length

= ___ × ___ × ___ = ___ blocks

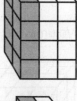

c) Number of blocks on one side = height × width

= ___ × ___ = ___ blocks

Total number of blocks = height × width × length

= ___ × ___ × ___ = ___ blocks

G6-31 Volume

> **Volume** is the amount of space taken up by a three-dimensional object.
>
> The objects shown here have a volume of 4 cubes.

1. Count the number of cubes to find the volume of the object.

   a)

   Volume = ____ cubes

   b)

   Volume = ____ cubes

   c)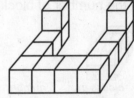

   Volume = ____ cubes

> We measure volume in cubic units or unit cubes. (The cubes are not drawn to scale.)
>
> $1 \text{ cm}^3 = 1$ cubic centimeter $1 \text{ m}^3 = 1$ cubic meter $1 \text{ in}^3 = 1$ cubic inch
>
> 1 cm / 1 cm / 1 cm   1 m / 1 m / 1 m   1 in / 1 in / 1 in

2. Find the volume of the object made from unit cubes. Include units in your answer.

   a) ↕1 ft

   Volume = ___5 ft³___

   b) ↕1 cm

   Volume = _____

   c) ↕1 mm

   Volume = _____

   d) 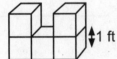 ↕1 ft

   Volume = _____

   e) 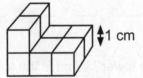 ↔ 1 in

   Volume = _____

   f) 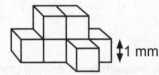 ↕1 m

   Volume = _____

   g) 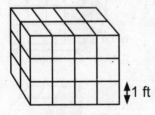 3 m

   Volume = _____

   h) 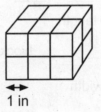 4 cm

   Volume = _____

   i) 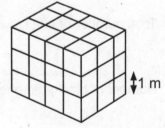 4 in

   Volume = _____

Mathematicians call rectangular boxes **rectangular prisms**. For a rectangular prism:

volume = length × width × height   OR $V = l \times w \times h$

3. Find the volume of the prism.

a) Length = ___3 m___

   Width = ___2 m___

   Height = ___5 m___

   Volume = ___3 m × 2 m × 5 m___ = ___30 m³___

   (box labeled: 3 m, 5 m, 2 m)

b) Length = _____

   Width = _____

   Height = _____

   Volume = _____ = _____

   (box labeled: 2 cm, 3 cm, 2 cm)

c) Length = _____

   Width = _____

   Height = _____

   Volume = _____ = _____

   (box labeled: 3 in, 4 in, 2 in)

d) Length = _____

   Width = _____

   Height = _____

   Volume = _____ = _____

   (box labeled: 4 ft, 9 ft, 4 ft)

e) l = _____

   w = _____

   h = _____

   V = _____ = _____

   (box labeled: 6 mm, 10 mm, 2 mm)

f) l = _____

   w = _____

   h = _____

   V = _____ = _____

   (box labeled: 3 m, 6 m, 2 m)

g) l = _____

   w = _____

   h = _____

   V = _____ = _____

   (box labeled: 12 in, 12 in, 12 in)

h) l = _____

   w = _____

   h = _____

   V = _____ = _____

   (box labeled: 40 ft, 65 ft, 100 ft)

4. Find the volume of the rectangular prism.

a) length 25 m, width 4 m, height 6 m

   Volume = _____

b) length 15 ft, width 40 ft, height 35 ft

   Volume = _____

5. a) One Chase Manhattan Plaza tower in New York City, NY, is a rectangular prism 86 m long, 37 m wide, and 248 m tall. What is the volume of the tower?

   b) Cheung Kong Center Tower in Hong Kong, China, is a rectangular prism 46 m wide, 46 m long, and 283 m tall. What is the volume of the tower?

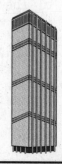

G6-32 Volume of Boxes with Fractional Sides

1. Roxanne has a box that is 1 inch long, 1 inch wide, and 1 inch tall.

   She packs the box with $\frac{1}{2}$ inch cubes.

   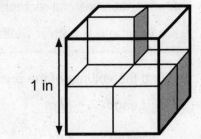

   a) How many cubes fit along each side of the box?

   Length = _____ cubes

   Width = _____ cubes

   Height = _____ cubes

   b) How many cubes does Roxanne need to fill the box? _____

   c) What is the volume of the box? _____ in³

   d) Use your answers to parts b) and c). What is the volume of each $\frac{1}{2}$ inch cube? ☐ in³

   e) The small cube has length = width = height = $\frac{1}{2}$ in.

   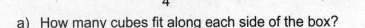

   Volume of the small cube = length × width × height = ☐ × ☐ × ☐ = ☐ in³

   f) Are your answers in parts d) and e) the same? _____

2. Tony also has a box that is 1 inch long, 1 inch wide, and 1 inch tall.

   He packs the box with $\frac{1}{4}$ inch cubes.

   a) How many cubes fit along each side of the box?

   Length = _____ cubes

   Width = _____ cubes

   Height = _____ cubes

   b) How many cubes does Tony need to fill the box? _____

   c) What is the volume of the box? _____ in³

   d) What is the volume of each $\frac{1}{4}$ inch cube? ☐ in³

   e) The small cube has length = width = height = $\frac{1}{4}$ in.

   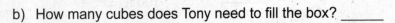

   Volume of the small cube = length × width × height = ☐ × ☐ × ☐ = ☐ in³

   f) Are your answers in parts d) and e) the same? _____

   g) What is the volume of 37 small ($\frac{1}{4}$ inch) cubes? _____

A cube with sides of $\frac{1}{4}$ inch has volume $\frac{1}{4}$ in $\times$ $\frac{1}{4}$ in $\times$ $\frac{1}{4}$ in $=$ $\frac{1}{64}$ in³. $\frac{1}{4}$ in ↕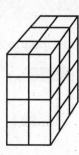

3. Martina made a rectangular prism from $\frac{1}{4}$ inch cubes.

   a) What are the dimensions of Martina's prism in inches?

   Length = _____   Width = _____   Height = _____

   What is the volume of Martina's prism? = ☐ × ☐ × ☐ = ☐

   b) How many $\frac{1}{4}$ inch cubes are in the prism? _____ × _____ × _____ = _____

   Find the volume of Martina's prism using the volume of one cube.

   Volume = _____ × $\frac{1}{64}$ in³ = ☐ in³

   c) Did you get the same answer in parts a) and b)? If not, find your mistake.

4. Find the volume of the prism made from $\frac{1}{4}$ inch cubes.

   a)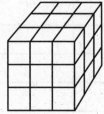

   Volume = _____

   b)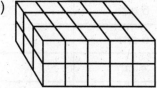

   Volume = _____

   c)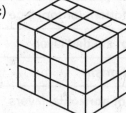

   Volume = _____

5. Find the volume.

   a)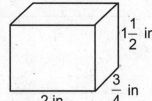
   $1\frac{1}{2}$ in
   $\frac{3}{4}$ in
   2 in

   Volume = _____

   b)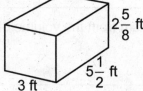
   $2\frac{5}{8}$ ft
   $5\frac{1}{2}$ ft
   3 ft

   Volume = _____

   c)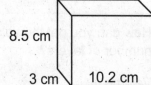
   8.5 cm
   3 cm   10.2 cm

   Volume = _____

6. Safety deposit boxes in a bank come in three sizes. Brian needs to store about 500 in³ of valuables. Which box out of the three below should he choose?

   Box A: 2.5 in × 5 in × 24 in   Box B: 3.5 in × 5 in × 24 in   Box C: $2\frac{1}{2}$ in × $10\frac{3}{8}$ in × 24 in

G6-33 Concepts in Volume

Flat surfaces on a 3-D shape are called **faces**.
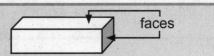 faces

1. Shade the top and the bottom faces of the prism.

a)   b) 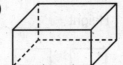   c)   d)

2. The bottom face of the rectangular prism shown has area 8 cm².

   What is the area of the shaded face? _____

3. These prisms are made from 1 cm³ cubes. Fill in the table.

Area of bottom (or top) face	6 cm²			
Volume of shaded layer	6 cm³			
Height of prism	4 cm			
Number of horizontal layers	4			
Volume of prism	24 cm³			

a) What do you notice about the number part of the area of the bottom (or top) face and the volume of the shaded layer?

_____

b) How can you get the volume of a prism from the volume of one layer and the number of layers?

Volume = _____

c) How can you get the volume of a prism from the area of the bottom (or top) face and the height of the prism?

Volume = _____

4. Find the volume of the prism.   a) 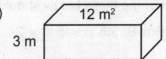   b)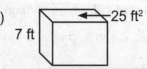

For rectangular prisms, volume = length × width × height   or   volume = area of top face × height.

5. Find the volume.

a)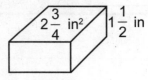

Volume = _____

b)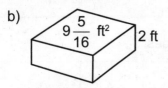

Volume = _____

c)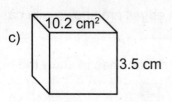

Volume = _____

d) Area of top face = 2.5 m²

Height = 3 m

Volume = _____

e) Area of top face = 200 mm²

Height = 45.5 mm

Volume = _____

f) Area of top face = 2.4 m²

Height = 3.2 m

Volume = _____

6. The structure was constructed from cubes. Find the volume of the structure.

a)

Volume = _____

b)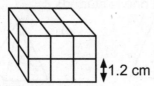

Volume = _____

c)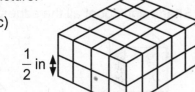

Volume = _____

📓 **BONUS ▶** Solve the problem in part c) a different way.

7. A rectangular tank is 35 cm long and 22 cm wide. The water height is 7.5 cm. Seth placed a stone in the tank and the water rose to a height of 10 cm. What is the volume of the stone?

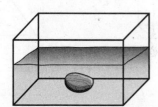

8. A prism has volume 72 in³. Its bottom face has area 12 in². What is the height of the prism? Write and solve an equation. Hint: volume = area of bottom face × height.

9. A rectangular tank is 80 cm long and 25 cm wide. The water height is 9.3 cm.

a) What is the volume of the water?

b) Marissa placed four cubes into the water. They are each 10 cm × 10 cm × 10 cm. What is the new volume of the contents of the tank?

c) What is the height of the water in the tank after Marissa added the cubes?

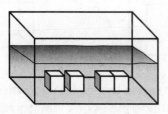

G6-34 Vertices, Edges, and Faces

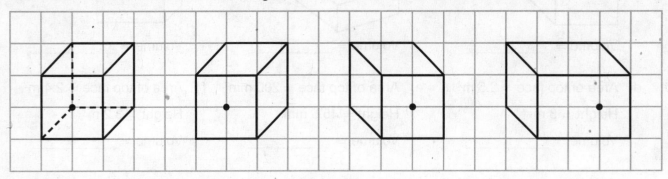

Faces meet at **edges**.

Hidden edges are shown with dashed lines.

hidden edges ← edges

1. Draw dotted lines to show the hidden edges.

2. Shade and count all the edges (the first one is started).

   a)

   _____ edges

   b)

   _____ edges

   c)

   _____ edges

   d)

   _____ edges

3. Edges meet at **vertices**. Draw a dot on each vertex. Count the vertices.

   a)

   _____ vertices

   b)

   _____ vertices

   c)

   _____ vertices

   d)

   _____ vertices

Edges and vertices of a shape make its **skeleton**. This is the skeleton of a cube.

4. Imagine the skeleton covered in paper and placed on a table. Shade the edges that would be hidden.

   a)

   b)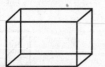

   c)

   d)

BONUS ▶ Imagine the skeleton covered in paper and hanging from the ceiling. Shade the edges that would be hidden when you look up at it.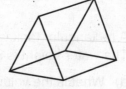

5. Shade the given face(s).

front face

a)   b)   c)   d)

back face

e)   f)   g)   h)

side faces

i)   j)   k)   l)

top and bottom faces

m)   n)   o)   p)

back face

q)   r)   s)   t)

bottom face

u)   v)   w)   x)

6. a) Fill in the table.

	Cube	Triangular Prism	Rectangular Prism	Triangular Pyramid	Rectangular Pyramid
Number of faces	6				
Number of edges	12				
Number of vertices	8				

b) Which two shapes in the table have the same number of faces, edges, and vertices?

_____ and _____

G6-35 Prisms and Pyramids

Prisms have two identical opposite faces called **bases**.

The bases of **triangular** prisms are triangles.   The bases of **rectangular** prisms are rectangles.

 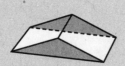   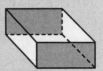

On rectangular prisms, any pair of opposite faces can be called bases.

1. Shade the bases of the prism. Then name the prism.

a)   b)   c)   d)

___triangular___

___prism___   _____   _____   _____

Pyramids have one base and a vertex opposite to the base.

The bases of **triangular** pyramids are triangles.   The bases of **rectangular** pyramids are rectangles.

Any face of a triangular pyramid can be called a base.

2. Shade the base and draw a dot on the vertex opposite the base. Then name the pyramid.

a) 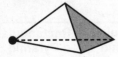   b)   c)   d)

___triangular___

___pyramid___   _____   _____   _____

3. Shade the base or the bases. Then name the prism or the pyramid.

a)   b)   c)   d)

_____   _____   _____   _____

_____   _____   _____   _____

4. a) Complete the table. Use actual 3-D shapes to help you.

Shape	Name	Number of ... Vertices	Edges	Faces	Picture of Faces
i)					
ii)					
iii)					
iv)					

b) Circle the bases in the last column of the table.

c) Count the number of sides in the base of each pyramid. Compare this number with the number of vertices in each pyramid. What do you notice?

_____

_____

d) Count the number of sides in the base of each prism. Compare this number with the number of vertices in each prism. What do you notice?

_____

_____

e) The faces that are not bases are called **side faces**.

The side faces of these prisms are _____.

The side faces of these pyramids are _____.

G6-36 Parallel and Perpendicular Edges and Faces

REMINDER ▶ We use arrows to mark parallel lines.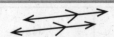

1. Mark the parallel edges on the 3-D shape.

   a)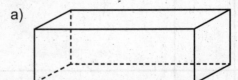

   b)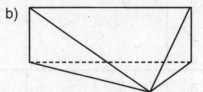

Edges can be parallel to a whole face.

Example: The thick edge is parallel to the shaded face.

---

2. a) Number the four edges parallel to the bottom face.

   b) Which of the edges that you numbered are parallel to each other?

   _____ and _____, _____ and _____

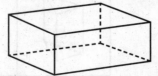

We use squares to mark perpendicular lines.

On a picture of a 3-D shape, some perpendicular lines do not look perpendicular.
For example, all angles on the faces of a cube are right angles.

---

3. Mark all the right angles on the 3-D shape.

   a)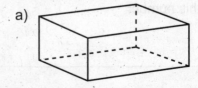

   b)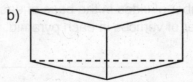

Edges can be perpendicular to faces, too.
When an edge is perpendicular to a face, it is perpendicular to all edges of that face.

The thick edge is perpendicular to the top face.   The thick edge is not perpendicular to the top face.

    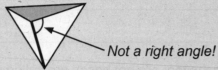   *— Not a right angle!*

---

4. Trace all the edges perpendicular to the shaded face.

   a) 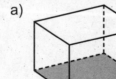   b) 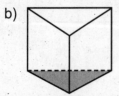   c) 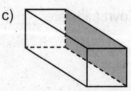   **BONUS** ▶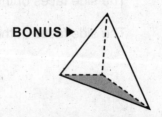

G6-37 Surface Area of Rectangular Prisms

1. Shade **all** the edges that have the same length as the edge marked.

Example:  ⟶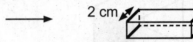

a)

b)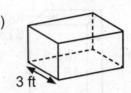

c)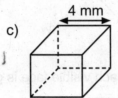

d)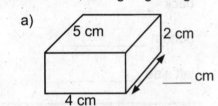

e)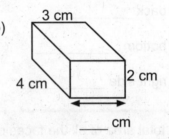

2. Find the missing edge length.

a)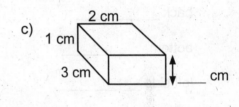
   _____ cm

b) _____ cm

c) _____ cm

3. a) Finish drawing the faces of the prism on the 1 cm grid.

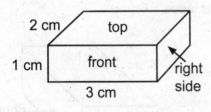

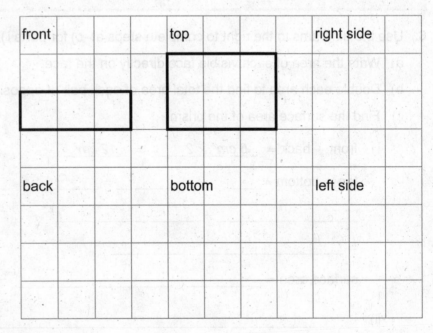

b) What is the area of each face of the prism?

front ___3 cm²___   top _____   right side _____

back _____   bottom _____   left side _____

c) What is the total area of all the faces of the prism? _____

4. Shade the face that has the same area as the already shaded face.

a)

b)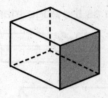

c)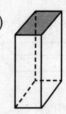

5. The area of each visible face is given. What is the area of each hidden face?

a)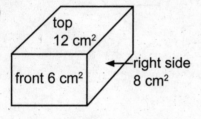

b)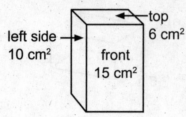

c)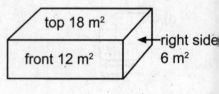

a) back _____

bottom _____

left side _____

b) back _____

bottom _____

right side _____

c) back _____

bottom _____

left side _____

The **surface area** of a 3-D shape is the total area of all the faces of the shape.

---

6. Use the diagrams to the right to complete steps a)–c) for parts i) and ii).

a) Write the area of each visible face directly on the face.

b) Double each area to find the total area of each pair of opposite faces.

c) Find the surface area of the prism.

i) front + back = ___6 cm² × 2___ = ___12 cm²___

top + bottom = _____ = _____

_____ + _____

= _____ = _____

surface area = _____ + _____ + _____ = _____

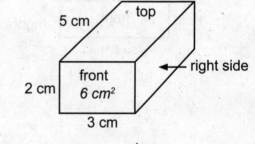

ii) _____

_____

_____

surface area = _____ + _____ + _____ = _____

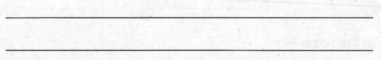

1. Mario traced all faces of a prism. Name the prism he traced.

a)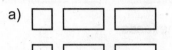

_____

_____

b)

_____

c)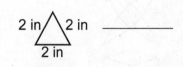

_____

REMINDER ▶ Faces that are not bases are called **side faces**. Side faces of prisms are rectangles.

---

2. Shade the bases of each 3-D shape and then sketch the faces in the chart.
Part a) is done for you.

	Shape	Bases	Side Faces
a)	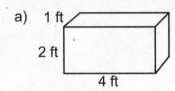		
b)			
c)			

3. How many of each face would you need to make these prisms?

a)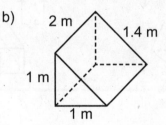

1 ft, 2 ft, 4 ft

4 ft / 2 ft _____

2 ft / 1 ft _____

4 ft / 1 ft _____

b)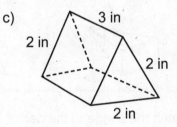

2 m, 1.4 m, 1 m, 1 m

1 m / 1.4 m / 1 m _____

2 m / 1 m _____

2 m / 1.4 m _____

c)

3 in, 2 in, 2 in, 2 in

2 in / 2 in / 2 in _____

3 in / 2 in _____

Mathematicians use small lines called hatch marks to show equal sides.

4. Rona traced all faces of the pyramid shown. Mark the equal sides on all the faces. Name the pyramid she traced.

a)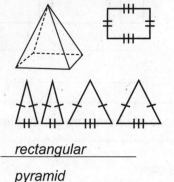

rectangular

pyramid

b)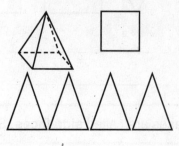

c)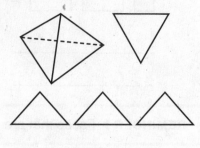

5. Shade the base or bases of the 3-D shape. Sketch the faces. Mark the equal sides on the faces.

a)

b)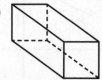

c)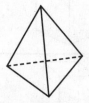

A **net** of a 3-D shape is a pattern that can be folded to make the shape. Examples:

| Rectangular Pyramid | Triangular Pyramid | Square Prism | Triangular Prism |

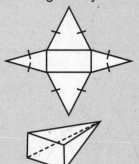  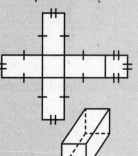

6. Match the shape to the net.

A.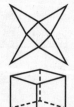

B.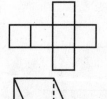

C.

D.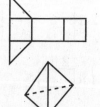

_____   _____   _____   _____

BONUS ▶ Mark the equal sides on the nets.

7. Mark the edges that come together when the net is folded with the same number. Then identify the 3-D shape.

a)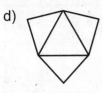

triangular _____

prism _____

b)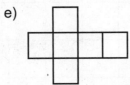

_____

_____

c)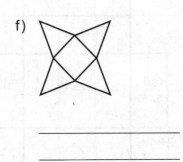

_____

_____

d)

_____

_____

e)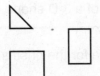

_____

_____

f)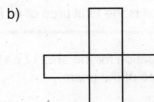

_____

_____

8. Circle the shape that could be the missing face for the net. Then add this face to the net.

a)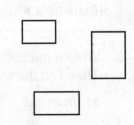

b)

9. Sketch a net for the 3-D shape. Mark the equal edges on your sketch.

a)

b)

c)

d)

BONUS ▶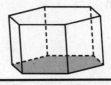

BONUS ▶ Sketch the faces for the hexagonal prism shown. (The shaded face is drawn for you.) Mark equal edges on the sketches.

G6-39 Nets and Surface Area of Rectangular Prisms

1. Draw a net for the prism on the grid below and label each face.

a)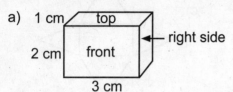

b)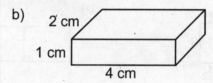

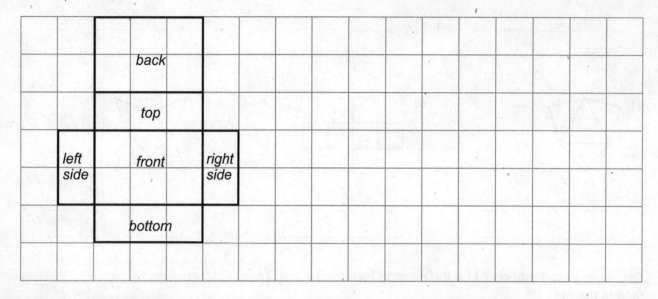

REMINDER ▶ Surface area is the total area of all faces of a 3-D shape.

2. Write a multiplication equation for the area of each face for the prisms in Question 1.
   Then find the surface area of the prism.

a) front ___2 × 3 = 6 cm²___

   back _____

   right side _____

   left side _____

   top _____

   bottom _____

   surface area of prism _____

b) front _____

   back _____

   right side _____

   left side _____

   top _____

   bottom _____

   surface area of prism _____

3. Draw a net for each prism on 1 cm grid paper. Then find the surface area of the prism.

a)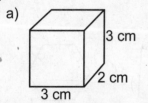

b)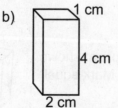

c)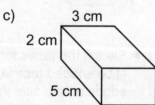

4. a) Label the net for the prism with the name of each face and the length of each edge.

i)
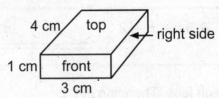

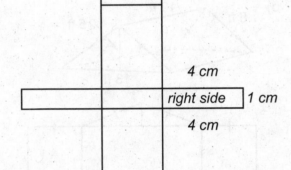
4 cm

right side | 1 cm

4 cm

ii)
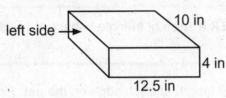

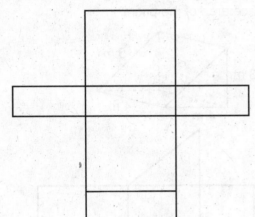

b) Find the area of each face. Include the units.

i) top ___ cm²   bottom _____

front _____   back _____

right side _____   left side _____

ii) top _____   bottom _____

front _____   back _____

right side _____   left side _____

c) Add the areas to find the surface area.

i) surface area _____

ii) surface area _____

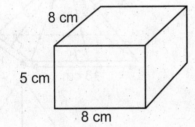
8 cm

5 cm

8 cm

5. a) Alexandra says that she only needs to find the area of two faces of this prism to calculate the surface area. Is she correct? Explain.

b) What is the surface area of the prism?

6. Ariel knows that the surface areas of the front, top, and right faces of a prism add to 20 cm². How can she find the total surface area of the prism? Explain.

7. Describe two different ways of finding the surface area of a rectangular prism. Which do you prefer?

8. Write a formula for the surface area of the prism using the length (*l*), width (*w*), and height (*h*).

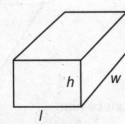
h | w

l

G6-40 Surface Area of Prisms and Pyramids

REMINDER ▶ Area of triangle = base × height ÷ 2   or $A = b \times h \div 2$

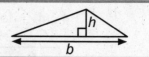

1. Write the length of each edge on the net. Find the area of each face. Then find the surface area of the prism.

a)

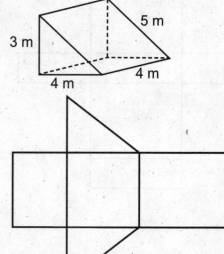

surface area = _____

b)

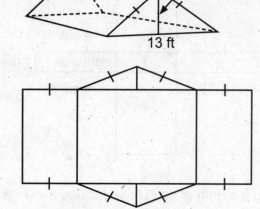

surface area = _____

2. Write the height and the base of each triangle on the net. Find the area of each face. Then find the surface area of the pyramid.

a)

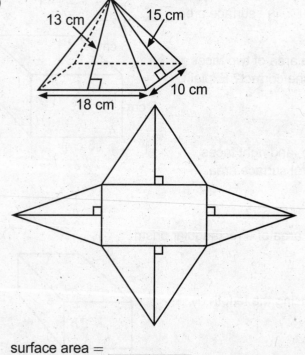

surface area = _____

b)

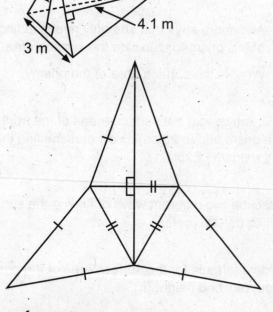

surface area = _____

G6-41 Volume and Surface Area (Advanced)

1. Find the surface area using any method.

a)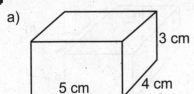
3 cm
5 cm
4 cm

b)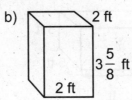
2 ft
$3\frac{5}{8}$ ft
2 ft

c)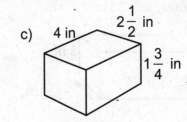
4 in
$2\frac{1}{2}$ in
$1\frac{3}{4}$ in

d)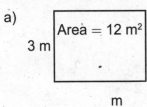
130 m
150 m
150 m

e)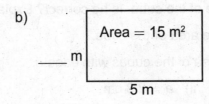
7 mm
8.6 mm
9.9 mm
7 mm

f) All edges are 5 in.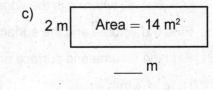
$4\frac{1}{3}$ in
5 in

2. A rectangular box is 30 cm long, 25 cm wide, and 20 cm tall.

a) Sketch the box. Write the dimensions of the box on your sketch.

b) Find the area of each face of the box.

c) The box has a lid. Mark it on your sketch. What are the dimensions of the face that is the lid?

d) Find the surface area of the box *without* the lid.

3. Find the missing length.

a)
Area = 12 m²
3 m
____ m

b)
Area = 15 m²
____ m
5 m

c)
2 m
Area = 14 m²
____ m

4. Write the formula for the volume of a rectangular prism using the area of the base and the height.

Volume of a rectangular prism = _____

5. a) Find the missing edge length.

i)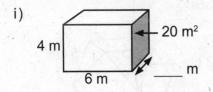
4 m
6 m
20 m²
____ m

ii)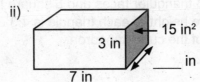
3 in
7 in
15 in²
____ in

iii)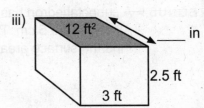
12 ft²
____ in
2.5 ft
3 ft

b) Find the volume and surface area of the prisms in part a).

6. Find the missing edge length.

a) Volume = 36 m³

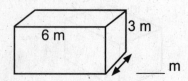

6 m   3 m   _____ m

b) Volume = 105 ft³

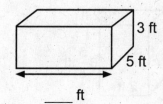

3 ft   5 ft   _____ ft

c) Volume = 21 in³

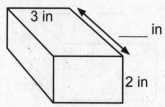

3 in   _____ in   2 in

7. A rectangular prism has volume 60 cm³. It is 5 cm long and 3 cm high.

a) Sketch the prism.

b) Find the missing dimension of the prism.

c) Find the surface area of the prism.

8. a) Aziz says that the volume of this box is 40 cm³. Is he correct? Explain why or why not.

b) Change the measurements of the box into centimeters and find the volume and the surface area. Hint: 1 m = 100 cm.

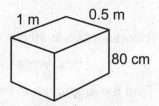

1 m   0.5 m   80 cm

9. Darya and Boris have a cube with edges $\frac{1}{2}$ ft.

a) Darya says she can find the volume of the cube using the formula

$V = a^3$, where a is the edge of the cube. Is she correct? Explain.

b) Boris says he can find the surface area of the cube using the formula $V = 6 \times a^2$, where a is the edge of the cube. Is he correct? Explain.

c) Find the volume and the surface area of the cube.

d) Find the volume and surface area of the cubes with edge a.

   i) $a = 3$ m   ii) $a = 2.8$ cm   iii) $a = 2\frac{3}{4}$ in

10. The Glass Pyramid at the entrance to the Louvre, in Paris, France, is a square pyramid. The sides of the base are 35 m long and the height of each side face is 27 m. How much glass was used to build the pyramid? Hint: Only the sides are made from glass.

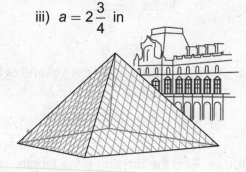

BONUS ▶ A cuboctahedron has 8 triangular faces and 6 square faces. All edges are 5 cm. The height of each triangle is 4.3 cm. Find the surface area of the cuboctahedron.

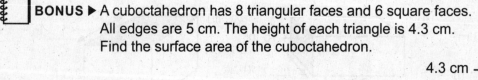

4.3 cm   5 cm

SP6-5 Histograms

Histograms represent data from sets.

- Histograms are made on a number line.
- The data points are divided into equal **intervals** and shown as side-by-side bars.
- The bars are the same width.
- The height of each bar shows how many data points are in each interval.

Example: **Length of Bird Songs**

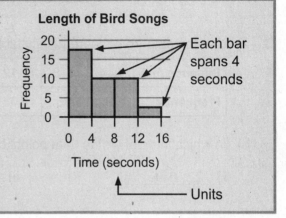

1. Use the histogram to fill in the blanks.

Length of Students' Favorite Songs

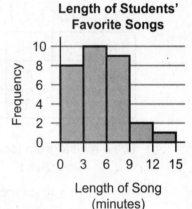

   a) How many intervals are shown? _____

   b) How long is each interval? _____ minutes

   c) How many songs are between 9 and 12 minutes long? _____

   d) The largest number of songs are between _____ and _____ minutes long.

   e) The longest songs are between _____ and _____ minutes long.

   f) What is the total number of songs reported on? _____ = _____

   g) How many songs were at least 6 minutes long? _____ = _____

2. Use the histogram to complete the frequency table and answer the questions.

Age (years)	0–15	15–30	30–45	45–60	60–75
Frequency	50				

Ages of People Who Use the Community Pool

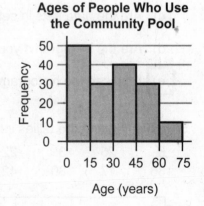

   a) In what unit is the data measured? _____

   b) How can you tell from the histogram that the intervals are all the same width?

   _____

   _____

   c) Using the histogram, can you tell the *exact* ages of the people who use the pool? Explain.

   d) If this data were shown on a dot plot, could you tell the pool users' *exact* ages? Explain.

When a data point falls on the boundary of an interval, it goes into the *higher* interval.

3. a) Use the data from the frequency table to draw a histogram.

Distance (mi)	0–4	4–8	8–12	12–16	16–20
Frequency	5	15	10	0	15

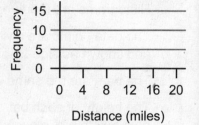

b) In which interval do the data points belong?

i) 2 __0–4__   ii) 8 _____   iii) 16 _____

4. a) Complete the frequency tables.

Set 1: ̶1̶, ̶1̶, ̶1̶, 7, 7, 7, 7, 12, 12, 16, 16

Hours	0–5	5–10	10–15	15–20
Tally	///			
Frequency	3			

Set 2: 4, 4, 4, 8, 8, 8, 10, 11, 15, 15, 19

Hours	0–5	5–10	10–15	15–20
Tally				
Frequency				

b) Draw a histogram for each set of data from part a).

Set 1

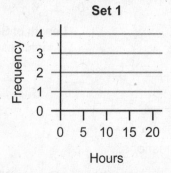

Set 2

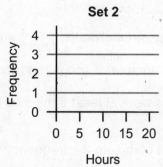

c) Are the data sets in set 1 and set 2 the same or different? _____

d) Are the histograms you drew the same or different? _____

e) How can the histograms be exactly the same when the data sets are different?

5. Finish putting the tallies into the frequency table.

̶8̶	̶2̶5̶	31	22	49	17	20	37	43	2	19	35	40
36	17	30	42	30	16	8	4	0	1	12	28	33

Interval	0–10	10–20	20–30	30–40	40–50
Tally	/		/		
Frequency					

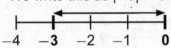

REMINDER ▶ The absolute value of a number is its *distance from 0.*

Examples: The absolute value of −3 is 3.   The absolute value of +4 is 4.

We write this as |−3| = 3.   We write this as |+4| = 4.

```
├──┼──┼──┼──┤                    ├──┼──┼──┼──┤
−4  −3  −2  −1   0                 0  +1  +2  +3  +4
```

1. How far is the number from 0?

   a) +3 is _____ units from 0.   b) −2 is _____ units from 0.   c) 0 is _____ units from 0.

2. What is the absolute value of the number?

   a) |+7| = __7__   b) |−16| = _____   c) |+3| = _____   d) |−124| = _____

Every data point in a set is a certain distance from the mean of that set. The **absolute deviation** of a data point is its distance *from the mean* without regard to direction.

Example: The mean of the set 0, 6, 9 is 5.

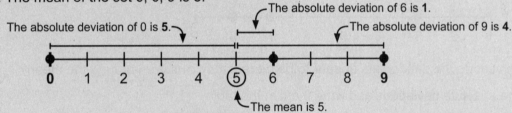

The absolute deviation of 6 is **1**.
The absolute deviation of 0 is **5**.
The absolute deviation of 9 is **4**.

The mean is 5.

3. The mean of the set 1, 2, 4, 6, 7, 11, 12 is 6.

   Mark the points on the number line. Find the absolute deviation of each data point, draw and label a line to show the absolute deviation (as shown for data point 1), and write it in the table. The first number in the set, 1, is done for you.

*The absolute deviation of 1 is **5.***

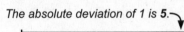

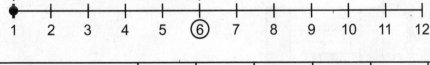

Data Point	1	2	4	6	7	11	12
Absolute Deviation	5						

The **mean absolute deviation**, **MAD**, shows how spread out the data points in a set are around the mean. It is the *average* of all the absolute deviations of the data points.

Example: The mean of the set 4, 8, 9 is 7.

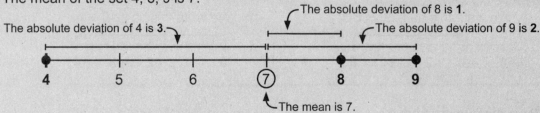

The absolute deviation of 8 is **1**.

The absolute deviation of 4 is **3**.

The absolute deviation of 9 is **2**.

The mean is 7.

$$\text{Mean absolute deviation} = \frac{3 + 1 + 2}{3} = \frac{6}{3} = 2$$

Mean absolute deviation is a measure of the **variability** of the data in a set.

4. Set 1 and set 2 both have three data points as shown on the number lines.

a) Find and circle the mean of each set, as in the grey box above.

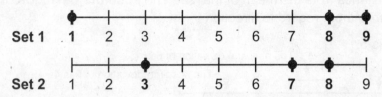

b) In which set do the data points appear to be more tightly clustered around the mean? _____

c) Find the absolute deviations and write them in the table.

Set 1

Data Point	1	8	9
Absolute Deviation			

Set 2

Data Point	3	7	8
Absolute Deviation			

d) Find the mean absolute deviation for each set. Set 1:   Set 2:

e) For which set is the MAD greater, set 1 or set 2? _____

f) Which data set is more tightly clustered around the mean, the one with the higher MAD or the one with the lower MAD? _____

5. The histograms show the marks of two classes on a test. Which class do you expect to have a higher MAD? Explain.

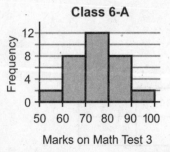

Marks on Math Test 3

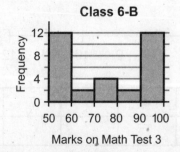

Marks on Math Test 3

SP6-7 Interquartile Range

The median of an ordered set divides the data into a **lower half** and an **upper half**.
The median of the lower half is called the **first quartile**, or **Q1**. The median of the upper half is called the **third quartile**, or **Q3**.

This is how to find Q1 and Q3 when a set has an *even number* of data points:

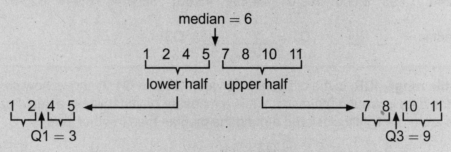

1. Label the median (M), the first quartile (Q1), and the third quartile (Q3), and mark each position with an arrow.

   a) 2 9 9 15 19 22 24 31

      Q1   M   Q3

   b) 3 3 6 6 14 18 18 20 21 23 23 25

   c) 20 22 22 28 33 35 35 39 40 40

   d) 1 1 1 3 4 4 4 4 4 7 7 7 8 9

2. Find the median, Q1, and Q3.

   a) 10 20 30 40 50 60 70 80   median = _____   Q1 = _____   Q3 = _____

   b) 1 2 6 8 13 15 17 18 27 29 44 45   median = _____   Q1 = _____   Q3 = _____

   BONUS ▶ 0 5,637 5,639 48,921 48,923 73,006 73,008 121,999

   median = _____   Q1 = _____   Q3 = _____

When a set has an *odd number* of data points, leave out the median when finding the quartiles.

Example: median = 17

        7 11 12 14 16   17   20 27 29 30 34
           lower half   upper half

   7 11 12 14 16 ←   → 20 27 29 30 34
        Q1 = 12   Q3 = 29

3. Find the median, Q1, and Q3.

a) 10 11 15 17 21 24 36 40 49

median = ____   Q1 = ____   Q3 = ____

b) 24 29 30 33 36 37 42 48 49 53 60

median = ____   Q1 = ____   Q3 = ____

BONUS ▶ 3,248 7,998 8,000 10,201 24,399 45,607 56,944 76,944 82,787

median = _____   Q1 = _____   Q3 = _____

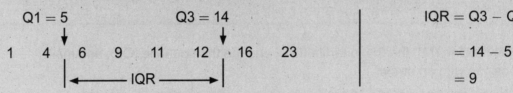

The **interquartile range**, **IQR**, is the difference between Q3 and Q1. It shows how spread out the *middle half* of the data is around the *median*. It is a measure of variability in a set of data. In some sets, the data points are more tightly clustered around the median than in other sets.

Example: Q1 = 5   Q3 = 14   IQR = Q3 − Q1

1   4   6   9   11   12   16   23   = 14 − 5

◀—— IQR ——▶   = 9

4. a) Use the dot plot to write the data as a list. Part i) has been started for you.

i)
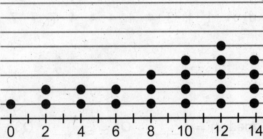

0 2 2 4 _____

_____

_____

ii)
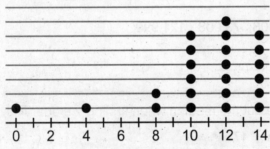

_____

_____

_____

b) Find Q1 and Q3 in each list. Mark them on the number line using arrows.

c) Find the interquartile range of each set from part a).

i) _____   ii) _____

d) Which data set has a greater IQR, i) or ii)? _____

e) Which data set is clustered more tightly around the median, i) or ii)? _____

5. Find Q1, Q3, and the IQR of the data.

a) 7 9 13 14 18 21 27 30   Q1 = __11__ Q3 = __24__ IQR = __24 – 11 = 13__

b) 48 58 68 78 88 98 108 118 128 138 148   Q1 = _____ Q3 = _____ IQR = _____

BONUS ▶ 489 4,531 4,533 19,888 27,714 68,755 68,757 85,004

Q1 = _____   Q3 = _____   IQR = _____

6. a) Find the IQR.

	Data	IQR
Set 1	0, 7, 8, 9, 10, 15, 16, 17, 18, 19, 20	
Set 2	0, 11, 12, 13, 14, 15, 16, 17, 18, 19, 20	
Set 3	0, 1, 2, 3, 4, 15, 16, 17, 18, 19, 20	

b) In which set are the data points most tightly clustered around the median? _____

c) In which set are the data points least tightly clustered around the median? _____

7. Find the missing values.

	Q1	Q3	IQR
Set 1	15	27	
Set 2	152	153	
Set 3	2		100
Set 4	30		2
Set 5		90	5
Set 6		379	18

BONUS ▶ Seamus thinks that two completely different data sets cannot have the same interquartile range. Is he correct? Explain.

_____

_____

_____

SP6-8 Box Plots

Box plots summarize data from sets. They are made on a number line and show five pieces of information about the set.

In the example on the right:
- the lowest value is 2
- Q1 is 4
- the median is 8
- Q3 is 10
- the highest value is 14

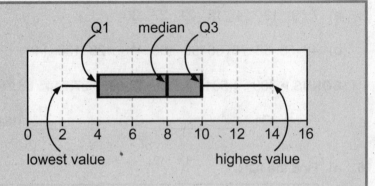

1. Use the box plot to find the median, the IQR, and the range.

a)

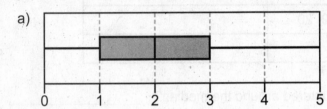

median = _____   IQR = _____

range = _5 − 0 = 5_____

b)

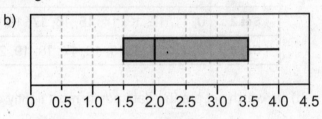

median = _____   IQR = _____

range = _____

c)

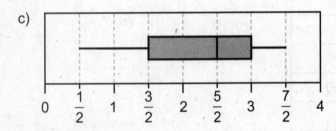

median = _____   IQR = _____

range = _____

d)

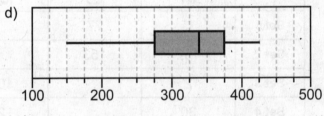

median = _____   IQR = _____

range = _____

2. Box plots A and B represent sets that have 100 data points.

a) Which box plot has the greater range, A or B? _____

b) Which box plot has the greater IQR? _____

c) In which box plot are the data points more tightly clustered around the median? _____

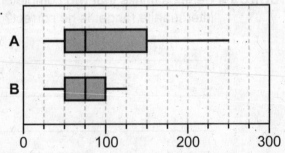

3. Students in a Sixth Grade and an Eighth Grade class recorded how many words they typed in one minute. Each box plot represents one of the grades.

a) Complete the table for box plot A and then box plot B.

	Q1	Q3	IQR
Box Plot A			
Box Plot B			

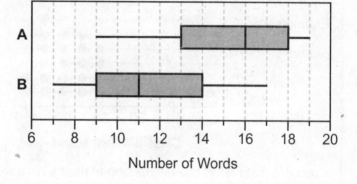
Number of Words

b) Do the IQRs help you determine which box plot represents which grade? Explain.

c) Do Q1 and Q3 help you determine which box plot represents each grade? Explain.

d) Box plot A represents _____ grade data.

Box plot B represents _____ grade data.

4. Match the dot plots to the box plots below. The dot plots all have 40 data points.

a)
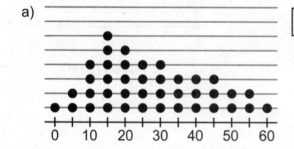
☐

b)
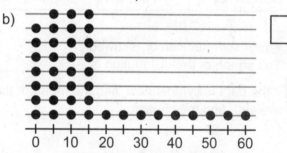
☐

c)
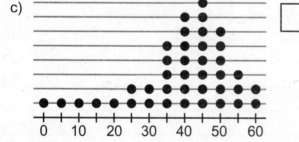
☐

d)
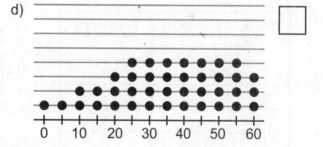
☐

A
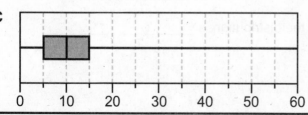

B
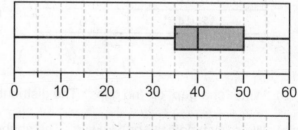

C
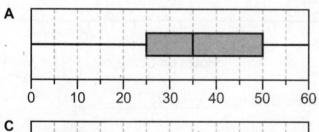

D
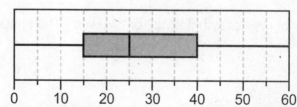

SP6-9 Distributions

The **distribution** of a set of data shows how the data points are arranged. We graph the data to see the shape of the distribution.

Examples:

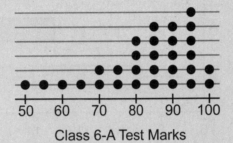

Class 6-A Test Marks

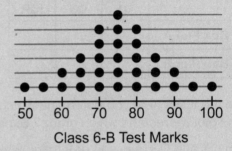

Class 6-B Test Marks

Each dot plot shows the distribution of marks on a test, one for Class 6-A and one for Class 6-B. The Class 6-A distribution is **skewed** and the Class 6-B distribution is **symmetrical**.

1. a) Use the data to make a dot plot.

Miles Walked	1	2	3	4	5
Frequency	1	2	5	2	1

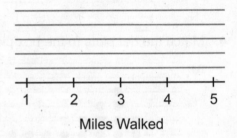

1   2   3   4   5

Miles Walked

b) Write "symmetrical" or "skewed":
The shape of the distribution is _____.

c) If the data is symmetrical, find the mean. If the data is skewed, find the median.

2. a) Use the data to make a histogram.

Hours on Computer	Frequency
0–2	1
2–4	0
4–6	2
6–8	4
8–10	6
10–12	7
12–14	6

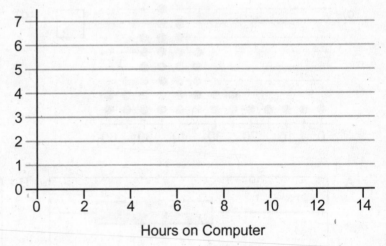

Hours on Computer

b) Write "one **gap**" or "no gaps": The distribution of the data has _____.

c) Write "symmetrical" or "skewed": The shape of the distribution is _____.

3. The dot plots show the number of books that students in six different classes at East Hill Elementary School read last year. Match the dot plot to one of the descriptions.

A symmetrical   **B** two gaps   **C** symmetrical with two gaps

D skewed   **E** skewed with an **outlier**   **F** no **peak**

a)

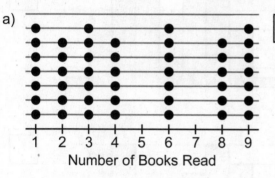

B

b)

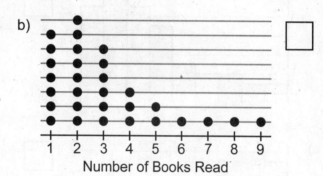

c)

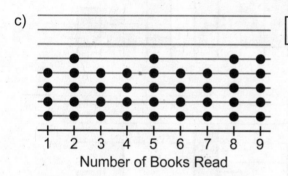

d)

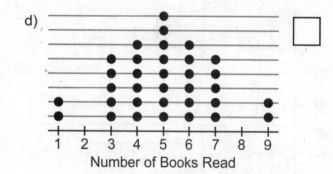

e)

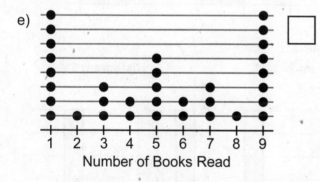

f)

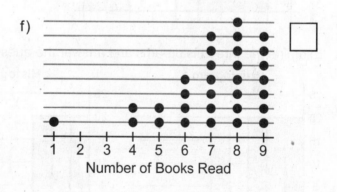

4. For which dot plots above could you find both the mean and median *without* doing any calculations? Explain.

_____

_____

_____

5. Match the histogram to one of the descriptions.

A symmetrical   **B** one gap   **C** skewed with an outlier

D two peaks   **E** skewed   **F** two gaps

a) 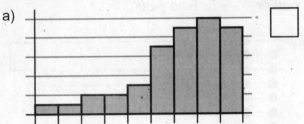 ☐

b) 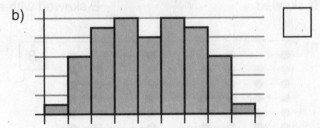 ☐

c) 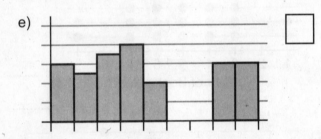 ☐

d) 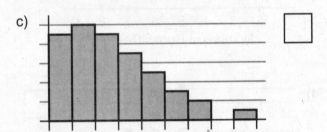 ☐

e) 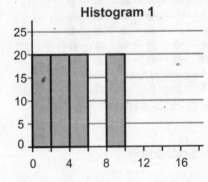 ☐

f) 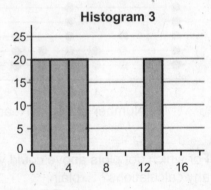 ☐

6. Examine the three histograms and answer the questions.

Histogram 1   **Histogram 2**   **Histogram 3**

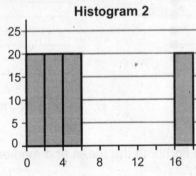

a) In which histogram will the mean and median be closest to each other? Explain.

_____

_____

b) In which histogram will the mean and median be farthest from each other? Explain.

_____

_____

7. The table shows the number of birds of different weights that Roz saw at the bird park on Sunday.

Weight (g)	5	6	7	11	12	17	120
Tally	⟊⟊⟊ III	⟊⟊⟊ I	⟊⟊⟊	I	II	II	I
Frequency							

a) Fill in the frequencies.

b) Calculate the mean.   mean = _____

c) Find the median.   median = _____

d) Mark the mean and median on the number line of the dot plot with arrows.

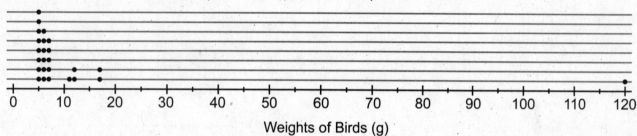

Weights of Birds (g)

e) Calculate what the mean would be if the outlier was at 70 and not 120.   mean = _____

f) Find what the median would be if the outlier was at 70 and not 120.   median = _____

g) Calculate what the mean would be if the outlier was at 520 and not 120.   mean = _____

h) Find what the median would be if the outlier was at 520 and not 120.   median = _____

i) Does changing the position of the outlier change the mean? _____

j) Does changing the position of the outlier change the median? _____

k) If you calculated the mean for only the data from 5 to 17, would the mean increase or decrease?

_____

l) Find the mean of the data from 5 to 17 to check your prediction in part k).

m) Find the median of the data from 5 to 17.

n) Explain why only the mean changed when you left out the outlier.